Portrait of Malik Ambar (Mughul, ca. 1620–30)
Courtesy of the Museum of Fine Arts, Boston (17.3103)

THE
AFRICAN PRESENCE
IN ASIA

*Consequences
of the East African
Slave Trade*

JOSEPH E. HARRIS

Northwestern University Press
Evanston
1971

Joseph E. Harris is Professor of History
at Williams College.

To Rosemarie, Joanne,
and Joseph Earl

CONTENTS

Preface   vii

Introduction   xi

1. Points of Origin   3
2. The Sea Voyage, Slave Marts, and Dispersion in Asia   27
3. The Volume of the Trade   43
4. Restriction and Abolition   51
5. Provinces of Freedom   65
6. Africans in Asian History   77
7. Malik Ambar: African Regent-Minister in India   91
8. Siddi Risala: A Community of African Descent in Hyderabad   99
9. Toward Assessing the Afro-Asian Heritage   115
   Appendix 1. Slave Statements   129
   Appendix 2. List of African Slaves Captured in Cutch, 1841   135
   Bibliographical Essay   139
   Index   147

Map 1. East Africa   4
Map 2. Scope of the East African Slave Trade   28

PREFACE

THIS BOOK evolved from my participation as chairman and commentator on a panel, "The African Abroad, or the African Diaspora," at the International Congress of African Historians hosted by Tanzania in 1965, which was attended by delegates from Africa, America, Asia, and Europe. The main paper on the African diaspora, read by Professor George Shepperson of the University of Edinburgh, had an enthusiastic reception and stimulated a lively and substantive discussion.[1] What especially impressed me, however, was the almost complete lack of information on the dispersion of Africans in Asia. I particularly recall that one of the very few references to the subject was the assertion by one delegate that African immigrants in Asia had been absorbed into the local societies. As an Afro-American I no doubt received that statement with the kind of skepticism nourished by the racial situation in the United States. However, neither I nor any other delegate even suggested to the conference that denigratory stereotypes of black people had developed in parts of Asia or that communities of African descent had emerged there. I left the conference with the belief that more should be known about the African experience in Asian history.

After a fairly intensive investigation of various library collections,

1. George Shepperson, "The African Abroad, or the African Diaspora," in *Emerging Themes of African History: Proceedings of the International Congress of African Historians*, ed. T. O. Ranger (Nairobi, 1968), pp. 152–76.

vii

I could document only a few aspects of the slave trade from Africa to Asia, a few revolts by African slaves, and the appearance of scattered Africans at Asian courts. There were virtually no detailed accounts of any of these subjects. I therefore sought funds for an exploratory research trip to Europe, Africa, and Asia to accomplish two objectives. First, I hoped to locate data that would be useful in reconstructing the African presence in Asian history. Second, I wanted to determine whether or not any communities of African ancestry exist in Asia. If communities of African descent could be found, they should be studied; if none was found, the reasons for and results of African assimilation should represent a challenging and rewarding research project.

I am most grateful for the support I received from the State University of New York, College at New Paltz; for a State University of New York Faculty Research Fellowship; and for a modest grant from the New York State Department of Education. With that support I was able to conduct research in England, Iran, and India during 1967 and 1968. Then and on other occasions I also collected materials and consulted with persons in Ethiopia.

I concluded that, if the study I wanted to write were to stimulate other scholars and writers to further research on this subject, I must identify a sufficient volume of resources and produce some convincing evidence that such a study could be undertaken in greater detail and would be worthwhile. I became increasingly encouraged that this would be possible, as leads took me to Tehran, Isfahan, Shiraz, and Bandar Abbas in Iran, and to New Delhi, Bombay, Hyderabad, and Ahmadabad in India. I examined the usual kinds of archival materials and recorded a great deal of oral testimonies. This book contains the results of those efforts. However, I have neither uncovered all the relevant sources nor collected all the substantive data. I therefore do not regard this book as even approaching a comprehensive study of African migrations and activities in Asia or even India, where I did most of my work. Rather, I present this as an exploratory work which may point the way for others to contribute to a more definitive effort.

Many people have contributed to this book, and I want to express my deep appreciation to them: in the *United States*, Professor Franklin D. Scott, Northwestern University; Professors Herman Walker and Peter Wright, State University of New York, College at New Paltz; in *Iran*, Professor E. Bastani-Parizi, Tehran University; Professor Terence O'Donnell, Paklovi University, Shiraz; Mr. Edward White, former Peace Corps Director, Tehran; Mr. Lenny Hines, former Peace Corps Volunteer, Kerman; Dr. Pakrovani, Red Lion and Sun Organization, Bandar Abbas; in *India*, Dr. P. K. Banerjee, former Indian Minister at Washington; Professor Anirudha Gupta, Indian School of International Studies; Professor H. K. Sherwani, Hyderabad; Mrs. S. Sadiq Ali, Indian Council for Africa; Dr. Hans Kruse, Visiting Professor, Osmania University, Hyderabad; Dr. William Mulder, former Director of the American Studies Research Center, Osmania University; Mr. Feroze Khan, interpreter, Hyderabad; Colonel Afsar Ali Baig, Records Office, Non-Indian States Forces, Hyderabad; Mr. Marzeur Rahman, Assistant, University of Bombay Library; Mr. Shri Parnlakar, Senior Assistant, University of Bombay Library; in *Pakistan*, Professor Iftikhar Ahmad Ghauri, Research Society of Pakistan, Lahore; Professor A. B. M. Habibullah, University of Dacca, East Pakistan.

I also benefited from the wise counsel of Professor George Shepperson, whose important work in the study of the African diaspora to the Western world is well known. I am further indebted to him for referring me to Professor V. G. Kiernan, whose suggestions of places and persons to see in India were most valuable. His recommendation of Professor Mohibbul Hasan, of the Jamia Millia Islamia in New Delhi, proved invaluable. Professor Hasan's knowledge of Islam, the Deccan, and present-day India made him one of my principal consultants. I have also had several most informative discussions with Professor Richard Pankhurst, of the Haile Sellassie I University in Addis Ababa.

I wish to thank the personnel at the India Records Office, London; the National Archives of India, New Delhi; the Archives and Secretariat Records Office, Elphinstone College, Bombay; the University of Bombay Library; the Andhra Pradesh State Archives, Hyderabad; the Records Office, Non-Indian State Forces, Hyderabad; the 1900 Fund and the library at Williams College, Williamstown, Massachusetts.

ix

The patient support of my wife and two children through this sometimes arduous task encouraged me to complete it. I cannot thank them enough.

Finally, I alone accept responsibility for the presentation and interpretation of the materials in this study.

INTRODUCTION

THIS IS a study of African migration to and settlement in parts of Asia, principally India. Such a study involves an examination of the immigrants' original and adopted homes as well as the areas through which they traveled during their migration. The history of Africans migrating to India was enriched by the enduring culture along the routes of passage — Arabia and the Persian Gulf. While the African made an impact on these areas, they also influenced him and to a great extent determined the kind of experiences he had in Indian history and culture.

Although there are few areas in the world where the African presence has not been felt, it is difficult to determine how many persons of African descent inhabit the world outside Africa. There are between 50 and 70 million in the Americas. How many more are scattered in other regions is a matter of conjecture; no doubt countless millions either are unaware of their African descent or do not wish to acknowledge it. The important point, however, is that throughout many centuries there has been a tremendous overseas dispersion of black people who have contributed significantly to the racial composition, culture, and history of their adopted homes.

The African diaspora, although global in dimension, cannot be dealt with in that perspective at the present time because of the very limited research that has been done in this field. It is regrettable that there are so few studies of the black diaspora and presence in the world, except for those about blacks in the United States. The body of literature about blacks in the Caribbean and in South America is growing; and it is probable that the small number of studies about blacks in Britain and France will increase.

For many years it has been generally thought that the Africans who migrated to Asia were absorbed into the local societies. While the Islamic world, which exercised considerable influence in both western and southern Asia and which was largely responsible for the involuntary migration of Africans to those areas, has always provided greater freedom for social mobility for black people than has the Christian world, it is also true that self-contained communities of African descent remain in parts of Turkey, Saudi Arabia, Yemen, Aden, Iraq, Iran, Pakistan, India, and other Asian countries. The fact that black people have remained in separate, isolated communities means that they have not been in the mainstream of the history of the countries in which they reside. Although those separate communities were not developed by deliberate legal machinery, as occurred in some Western countries, the attitudes and actions of many Asians and Afro-Asians have been influenced by the latter's general isolation from the dominant community. This has been the case despite the fact that the Afro-Asians' heritage includes substantial contributions to the history and culture of their adopted lands. The chapters that follow will show how those contributions have influenced the course of Asian and African history and human relations.

In addition to the geographical dimension, the African diaspora may also be studied in terms of time and stimuli. It is indeed possible to trace the African exodus back to prehistoric times and to analyze the implications of the idea that man originated in Africa and migrated abroad. The work of Dr. Louis Leakey poses this fascinating question: Are we all of African descent? But it is not the intention of this study to explore that issue or the exciting possibilities of overseas African influence which resulted from sea voyages in the Indian Ocean before Christ, a subject admirably introduced by the Soviet writer, Yu. M. Kobishanow.[1] There are other time dimensions which could be considered in the study of the African diaspora: the black

1. See Yu. M. Kobishanow, "On the Problem of Sea Voyages of Ancient Africans in the Indian Ocean," *Journal of African History*, VI, no. 2 (1965), 137–41.

slave in classical Greece and Rome; [2] the eighth-century occupation
of the Iberian peninsula by the Muslims, who implanted Africans
there and elsewhere in Europe; the European slave trade, followed by
colonial rule, which caused Africans to migrate both voluntarily and
involuntarily. These are all pertinent chapters of the African diaspora,
but this study is concerned with the Asian dispersion caused primarily,
though not exclusively, by the East African slave trade throughout
the late eighteenth and nineteenth centuries.

The East African slave trade long predated the Atlantic slave trade
and was principally conducted by Muslim Arabs. Unlike the Atlantic
slave trade, which has long attracted the attention of scholars and
popular writers, the Indian Ocean trade has not received much attention. Among the several possible reasons for this is the fact that the
trade from East Africa did not become the kind of big business that
developed in West Africa. Most of the Arabs were small dealers, usually trading such items as ivory, spices, and hides, all of which com-
peted with the trade in men. They normally transported only 10 to 25,
seldom more than 75 to 100, slaves at a time in their dhows. Only
rarely did they transport more than 200, well below the many hundreds transported in European vessels. Further, the disposal of African slaves in the Eastern world was generally at scattered points in
Asia: along the Red Sea and the Persian Gulf, in India, and possibly
beyond. There were a few small brokers, but none on the order of
those who emerged, for example, in the United States. Consequently,
since most of the Asian trade was small and conducted on a personal
basis, careful records were seldom kept. Moreover, since throughout
the nineteenth century the British sought to suppress the slave trade,
those who surreptitiously engaged in it avoided recordkeeping.

In addition to the problem of having only fragmentary documentation on the migration, the fact that many Africans in Asia adopted
Islam, Muslim names, and the Arabic language makes it difficult for
the historian to identify them. But much of the story can still be told.
There are many travel accounts written by Arabs and Europeans who
took notice of the slave trade and of Africans in Asia; there are a
few Arab documents by slave dealers; and, fortunately for the his-

2. See Frank M. Snowden, *Blacks in Antiquity* (Cambridge, Mass., 1970).

torian, there are numerous volumes left by the British East India Company dating back to the seventeenth century. In addition, during the nineteenth century there was an increase in the number of missionaries and others dispatched to investigate the East African slave trade; some of their reports are available. Portuguese documents reaching back to the sixteenth century are accessible in Goa, although they are not well catalogued. Other information has been preserved in local Asian languages, too little of which has come to the attention of present-day researchers. Finally, and of vital importance, there is the living evidence of the diaspora, the communities of African descent in several Asian countries. Since the East African slave trade continued into the twentieth century, many persons of African descent in Asia can recount the experiences they and their families have had and can explain the image they have of the dominant communities around them. Their genealogies are useful; and the places they name, in which they and their families have lived and through which they have traveled, are also revealing. These living specimens should not be overlooked in studying the diaspora, for their accounts can be of much value if examined carefully and critically.

The study of the African exodus to Asia and the extent of African absorption into the local societies will add to the much-needed body of literature on black people in the Eastern world in general and to African and Indian history in particular. It will also shed needed light on cross-cultural contact in countries where stigmas attached to black people seem less pronounced than in Western countries.

This study will also help destroy the myth that Africans were isolated, static, and uninvolved in the world prior to their contact with white men, with all the demeaning implications this view has had for race relations, past and present. Contact between Europeans and East Africans dates from the late 1480s, when Portuguese explorers rounded the southern tip of Africa; the relationship between the two groups did not develop seriously, however, until the height of the slave trade and then expanded into more legitimate, though still exploitative, activities in the latter half of the nineteenth century. Prior to this contact, Africans had not only developed viable societies at home but had contributed notably to historical developments in parts of Asia.

Perhaps the most important contribution this modest study can make will be to stimulate Eastern and Western scholars and professional writers to devote some of their energies to the reconstruction of the African heritage in Asia. Africanists and Asianists should be interested in this kind of study from the perspective of their several disciplines, because it overlaps both areas and therefore provides the kinds of relationships social scientists find helpful in understanding cross-cultural influences.

The African Presence
in Asia

1.
Points
of Origin

THE PERIPLUS, a Greek guidebook for navigators written sometime during the first century A.D., reported Arabs trading along the Somali coast for slaves. This activity increased with the establishment of Arab settlements along the coast in the early eighth century. Reginald Coupland thus contended that the slave trade was continuous from earliest times, with Arabs striking far inland by the time the trade reached its peak in the nineteenth century. G. S. P. Freeman-Grenville disagreed with Coupland and held that it was only after the Omani Arabs began intervening in East African affairs in the seventeenth century that slaves were exported from the East African coast south of the Horn of Africa (Somali region). He has explained that descriptions of revenues seldom mention slaves, and never are they mentioned as an export. Although slaves were exported from Zeila and Berbera, "there is no evidence to suggest that they were exported at all from the coast farther south during the sixteenth century or early seventeenth century."[1]

While Freeman-Grenville's criticism of Coupland's sweeping generalizations seems to have some validity, it is very doubtful that slaves were not exported at all from around the Zanzibar region until the seventeenth century. Indeed, Gervase Mathew, writing in the same book as Freeman-Grenville, speaks not only of the slaves who

1. G. S. P. Freeman-Grenville, "The Coast, 1498–1840," in *History of East Africa*, ed. Roland Oliver and Gervase Mathew (London, 1963), I, 152. See also Reginald Coupland, *East Africa and Its Invaders* (Oxford, 1938), pp. 17, 18.

3

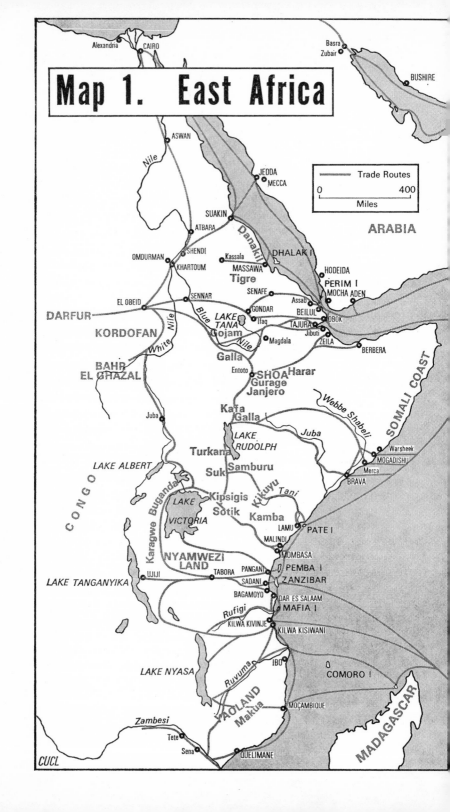

Map 1. East Africa

Trade Routes

0 — 400

Miles

Alexandria • CAIRO
Basra • Zubair
BUSHIRE

ASWAN
Nile

JEDDA
MECCA

SUAKIN
ATBARA
OMDURMAN • SHENDI • Kassala
KHARTOUM • MASSAWA
Sennar
Tigre
DHALAK I

ARABIA

Danakil

HODEIDA
PERIM I
MOCHA ADEN

EL OBEID • SENNAR
SENAFE
DARFUR
KORDOFAN
Blue
Gojam
LAKE TANA • Ifaq
GONDAR
Assab
BEILUL
OBOK
TAJURA
Magdala
Jibuti
ZEILA
BERBERA

White
Nile
Galla
BAHR EL GHAZAL

Entoto
SHOA • Harar
Gurage
Janjero

SOMALI COAST

Webbe Shabeli

Juba
Kafa
Galla I

LAKE RUDOLPH
Juba
Warsheek
MOGADISHU
Merca
BRAVA

CONGO

LAKE ALBERT
Turkana
Suk • Samburu

Karagwe
Buganda
LAKE VICTORIA
Kipsigis
Sotik • Kamba
Kikuyu
Tani

LAMU • PATE I
MALINDI
MOMBASA

NYAMWEZI LAND
UJIJI
TABORA
PANGANI
SADANI
BAGAMOYO
PEMBA I
ZANZIBAR

LAKE TANGANYIKA

Rufigi
DAR ES SALAAM
MAFIA I
KILWA KIVINJE
KILWA KISIWANI

LAKE NYASA
Ruvuma
IBO
COMORO I

YAOLAND
Makua
MOÇAMBIQUE

MADAGASCAR

Zambesi
Tete
Sena
QUELIMANE

CUCL

were exported from Opone (the southern Somali coast) to Egypt in ancient times but also of the Mesopotamian black slave-soldiers from East Africa; he indicates that the slave trade from the southern region was "probably a constant factor" on the coast between A.D. 100 and 1498. It is even possible that earlier than the fifteenth century, when one can document the arrival of a Chinese fleet at Mogadishu, the Chinese trade with East Africa included supplies of slaves.[2] The case of India is much clearer. The area of Gujarat, which was long in commercial contact with East Africa, and the Deccan (central India), which was ruled by the Bahmani kings, during whose reigns there was considerable use of African slave-soldiers, were pointed out by travelers in the Middle Ages as areas with substantial numbers of African slaves. Mathew believes that most of those slaves came from the area of present-day Tanzania.[3]

The slave trade in East Africa seems to have been small in over-all volume until the nineteenth century. The principal Asian demands were for workers on the date plantations in Basra, Bandar Abbas, Minab, and along the Batinah coast and in the pearl-diving industry in Bahrein and Lingeh on the Persian Gulf; slave-soldiers in various parts of Arabia, Persia, and India; dock workers and dhow crews in much of the Arab-controlled Indian Ocean; and concubines and domestic servants in Muslim communities throughout Asia. Except for the domestic servants, concubines, and soldiers, the slaves were usually used as gang labor.

The principal slave dealers were the Arabs, the Omani Arabs in particular. The Arabs called the northern Somali coast Ras Assir ("the cape of slaves"). The people of this area, converted to Islam by the thirteenth century, engaged in the slave traffic to the Muslim East. It appears that the establishment of Muslim Arab trading centers along the northern coast was accompanied by a great expansion of the slave commerce in the ports of Suakin, Dhalak, Zeila, Berbera, Mogadishu, Merca, Brava, Massawa, and Tajura. Some of these ports re-

2. C. Martin Wilbur, *Slavery in China during the Former Han Dynasty* (New York, 1967), p. 93; and E. Bretschneider, *On the Knowledge Possessed by the Ancient Chinese of the Arabs and Arabian Colonies* (London, 1871), pp. 13–22.

3. Mathew, "The East African Coast until the Coming of the Portuguese," in *East Africa*, ed. Oliver and Mathew, pp. 101, 121.

ceived slave caravans which originated in or passed through Ethiopia, where the institution of slavery was long recognized by the *Fetha nagast*, the Ethiopian code which was partly based on Mosaic law and which sanctioned the taking of slaves from among unbelievers.

Oman, which held a key position in the naval and commercial strategy of the Middle East, spearheaded the Arab involvement; and Muscat, the Omani capital, commanded the approach to the Persian Gulf, through which large numbers of African slaves were transported. Not until the eighteenth century, however, did Oman have any direct political involvement in East Africa. In 1784 Said ibn-Ahmad, a rival claimant to the Omani throne, went south with his son Ali to carve out an independent domain. Kilwa surrendered to Ali that year, and Zanzibar the next. From that time, Omani rulers claimed sovereignty over several towns on the East African coast and intervened on many occasions to assert their control over maritime trade. By 1804 French Captain P. Dallons in Zanzibar reported that the governor of Kilwa was paying the Omani sultan a large annual sum as dues on slaves. In 1806 Said ibn-Ahmad won absolute power in Oman and established firm rule in Zanzibar. During his reign Zanzibar became the main port for the East African slave trade and gradually developed as the center of Omani activities in East Africa generally. In 1811 British Capt. T. Smee, who sailed along the East African coast on orders from the Bombay government, reported that Zanzibar was an important market for slaves, exporting an estimated 6,000 to 10,000 annually to Muscat, India, and the Mascarene Islands.[4]

After Said established his position in Zanzibar, several of his compatriots decided to exploit the agricultural and commercial potential of East Africa. Cloves were introduced in 1818, and in the course of a few years large plantations developed. This created an increased demand for labor to clear the land, keep it worked, and harvest the crops twice a year or, in the case of the coconut palms producing copra, four times a year. There was consequently a tremendous demand for slaves, from both plantation owners and slave exporters on the islands of Zanzibar and Pemba, and during Said's regime the slave trade expanded remarkably. Traders increased in number on

4. Freeman-Grenville, "The Coast," pp. 156–58; and *Transactions of the Bombay Geographical Society*, VI (1884), 23–61.

the coast, new routes into the interior were established, deeper penetration toward the west occurred, and reports of slave caravans increased. Commercial expansion also resulted in part from the growing demand in Europe and America for gums, vegetable oils, ivory,
and slaves. East African slaves were made to carry ivory with them
from the interior, and on their arrival at the coast they and their
ivory were sold. This was indeed a lucrative business, especially for
the sultan, who became dependent on customs duties and taxes levied
on the slave trade.

A climactic point in the East African slave trade occurred in 1840,
when the sultan moved the capital from Muscat to Zanzibar, after
having defeated the Mazrui dynasty at Mombasa in 1837. This shift
strengthened the already well developed political and economic ties
between the two areas. A large part of East Africa thus came under
the direct rule of a sovereign who had established commercial and
diplomatic relations with the major Western powers. These powers
had important stakes in the region's commerce, particularly the slave
trade. Commercial treaties had been negotiated with the United States
in 1833, Britain in 1839, and France in 1844. Furthermore, the sultan,
realizing the tremendous economic potential of Zanzibar's clove plantations and the slave trade, was in a position to protect and promote
the expansion of both.

Much of the European demand for slaves was met in East Africa.
The first period of substantial demand occurred between 1642 and
1648, when the Dutch captured the Portuguese West African forts in
Angola and the Gold Coast. This greatly restricted the Portuguese
source of supply of slaves to Brazil; consequently, Mozambique, Portugal's East African colony, became a major source of bondsmen
until 1648, when the West African forts were recaptured. A second
period of important European demand occurred during the nineteenth
century. This resulted from a gradual limitation of the trade in the
Atlantic Ocean beginning in 1807, when both the United States and
England officially abolished the slave trade. Although it took decades
for the English to check the traffic effectively, the obstacles and ha-
rassment supplied by the British Slave Squadron in West Africa were
sufficient to cause many slavers to seek supplies from East Africa.
Although abolition was gradually applied to that region also, there
were never enough British cruisers to provide even the limited effec-

7

tiveness of the efforts in the Atlantic, and the Arab rulers and traders in East Africa were no more amenable to voluntary abolition than were their European and West African counterparts.

From the time of Napoleon's invasion of Egypt in 1798, European influence and control gradually spread over much of northern Africa and the Middle East. This trend and the simultaneous increase in abolitionist sentiment meant that the northern entrepôts of the trans-Saharan (mainly Tripoli and Benghazi) and Nile Valley slave trade to Asia were eventually drawn into the European orbit of trade in produce. This situation forced the Arab slave dealers to look to the East African coast to meet the Asian demand for slaves. Although the slave commerce of northern Africa did not end because of this shift in emphasis, it was greatly minimized in significance.

The demand for East African slaves was further stimulated by the development of a plantation economy based on slave labor in the French Indian Ocean colonies of Mauritius and Réunion — the Mascarene Islands. This development began around 1735, when Bertrand Franch Mahé de la Bourdonnais became governor general of the Mascarenes. There had previously been some slave trading with the Portuguese for Africans from Mozambique, Mombasa, and Madagascar. Bourdonnais encouraged the development of sugar and coffee plantations on the islands and sought to increase the supply of African labor. Together with his friend Nicolau Tolentino D'Almeida, governor of Mozambique, the French governor general set in motion a relationship on which a vigorous trade in Africans was developed. From 1735 to 1740 the Mascarene Islands imported 1,000 to 2,000 slaves from Mozambique; between 1781 and 1794 most of the 46,461 slaves who were exported from Mozambique were loaded on French vessels and presumably were shipped to the Mascarenes. Similar events were taking place in Kilwa. A Captain Morice, who visited Kilwa in 1776 to initiate contractual agreements for the sale and shipment of slaves to the French colonies, concluded a treaty with the sultan of Kilwa. The sultan, who received a duty on each slave, contracted to supply Morice with 1,000 slaves annually; that figure rose to a total of 4,193 for the years 1788–90.[5]

5. See Edward A. Alpers, *The East African Slave Trade* (Nairobi, 1967),

By the middle of the nineteenth century the French demand for slaves from East Africa had increased tremendously, primarily because of the abolition of slavery in all French colonies during the revolution of 1848. The French settlers in Réunion (Mauritius had been ceded to the British in 1814) therefore sought to meet the demand for labor on the plantations by importing workers from India. The supply from the French Indian possessions of Pondicherry and Karikal, however, was insufficient, and Britain denied the French permission to recruit in British India. Thus the French resorted to the *engagé* system, in which Africans were purchased to work in Réunion for five years. It was in this connection that M. Runtoné, a representative of some merchants in Réunion, appealed to Sultan Said Majid in 1858 for

> some slaves; young and strong, to labor in our colonies. . . . The profit shall be divided equally between me and your Highness. . . . The French Government has given permission to all the Governors of their colonies to purchase slaves and to set them free; for the Government of France desires the happiness of all mankind, so people should convey slaves to Bourbon [Réunion] to be taught labor in order that they may become wise and clever.[6]

On June 29, 1858, Baron Darrison, governor of Réunion, explained to the sultan of Zanzibar:

> The land of La Réunion is rich and fruitful, but the heat of the sun forbids white men from working there. That is why we turn to the black man God has made for these climates. . . . Afterwards they will be authorized to return to your country; they will have learnt the cultivation of sugar, they will have learnt our customs; they will then bring back to you a population able to cultivate your land and increase the source of the riches of your state.[7]

In August, 1858, Christopher Rigby, British consul at Zanzibar, informed the chief secretary to the government of India that the slave trade all along the East African coast was expanding to a far greater

---

pp. 6–7; and Charles E. B. Russell, *General Rigby, Zanzibar and the Slave Trade* (London, 1935), pp. 156, 368.

6. Bombay, Political Department, December 31, 1858, pp. 18, 20, 398.

7. *Ibid.*, p. 20.

degree than previously, that the prices were more than doubling, and that this was due to the French government's orders permitting the importation of slaves into the island of Réunion. Rigby wrote:

> I am informed by the merchants here [Zanzibar] that one person in Marseilles has contracted to land 25,000 negroes in the Island of Bourbon within the next two years. These negroes are purchased by native agents all along the Mozambique coast, and taken on board French ships.[8]

Rigby informed his foreign office that Frenchmen in East Africa bought Africans, took them to a judge and received papers nominally freeing them, and shipped them to Réunion. A French agent told Rigby that 10,000 of these laborers, who were referred to as *engagés*, were needed per year, a demand which affected both Zanzibar and Portuguese East Africa. Lord John Russell reported in 1861:

> Brigadier [W. M.] Coghlan estimates the number of slaves exported from the dominions of the Sultan of Zanzibar and from the neighboring Portuguese territories at upwards of 30,000 annually, and he states that whole districts have been depopulated, and towns and villages destroyed in the wars that have been carried on for the purpose of procuring slaves for exportation.[9]

The East African slave trade remained vigorous throughout the 1860s and into the 1870s. A decline occurred after 1873, when Britain and Zanzibar negotiated a treaty of abolition; but even that agreement did not stop the trade, which persisted into the twentieth century (see Chapter 4).

Sources and Collection
of Slaves

Although it is impossible to determine the areas of origin for all East African slaves, let alone the particular villages from which they came, several regional sources of supply can be indicated. It is very

8. Bombay, Secret Department, September, 1858, p. 21.
9. Great Britain, Foreign Office, Vol. 84 (*Slave Trade*, Vol. 1019), Russell to Rigby, February 19, 1861.

likely that the immediate hinterland of the entire eastern coast suffered losses at one time or another, and even inhabitants of coastal
cities fell victim to raids, kidnapings, and other means of capture.

It is well known that there was a considerable amount of slave trading in the eastern Sudan and all along the Nile Valley for many centuries. Nubia supplied many soldiers for Egyptian armies, and in
many cases Nubian slaves were used to pay Egyptian soldiers. As
late as the nineteenth century, there was a report of Egyptian soldiers
collecting 2,700 slaves in the Sudan and distributing the slaves among
themselves to cover wages.[10]

A rich source of slaves for Egypt was western Nubia, from where,
according to one estimate made in the nineteenth century, 12,000
to 15,000 slaves were exported annually. Slave traders in the western
region and in other parts of the eastern Sudan were, for the most
part, from Darfur or Kordofan. The Bahr el Ghazal region also was
long a major source of slaves for the Egyptian markets. Charles Gordon, the governor general of the Sudan, estimated that between 80,000
and 100,000 slaves were exported from the Bahr el Ghazal during
the years 1875–79.[11] Although Egypt is outside the main focus of this
study, it should be noted that several of the sources that supplied
Egyptian markets also provided slaves for the Red Sea ports of East
Africa.

The principal source for the slaves sold in the southern Red Sea
ports and along the northern Somali coast was the Gurage region
of Ethiopia. John Krapf, the German missionary, estimated that 3,000
slaves were exported from Gurage annually in the first half of the
nineteenth century. Antonio Cecchi calculated in the 1870s that Jimma,
in spite of restrictions on the trade, was one of the largest slave markets
in southwestern Ethiopia, handling about 4,000 a year. He also reported that another southwestern market, Bonga, exported an estimated 8,000 slaves annually in the 1870s. Gondar and Shoa and the
Bahr el Ghazal also supplied slaves for Ethiopian markets.[12]

10. *Irish University Press Series of British Parliamentary Papers* (Shannon,
1969), *Slave Trade*, LXXXVII, 455–58; and Richard Gray, *A History of the
Southern Sudan, 1839–1889* (Oxford, 1961), p. 68.

11. G. B. Hill, *Colonel Gordon in Central Africa* (London, 1887), p. 369.

12. Richard Pankhurst, "The Ethiopian Slave Trade in the Nineteenth and
Early Twentieth Centuries: A Statistical Inquiry," *Journal of Semitic Studies,*

South of the Horn, the major sources of slaves were the Great Lakes and Congo regions. Traders traveled up the Tana River to Mount Kenya, where they collected slaves from various centers. In the more western regions, caravans were assembled in Masailand, Sotik, Kipsigis, and around Lake Victoria. Some merchants, notably the Kimaneta, traded north into Suk and Turkana country and as far as Lake Rudolf. From the 1830s to the 1880s Baganda traders under Kabakas (Baganda kings) Suna and Mutesa collected slaves on the eastern shore of Lake Victoria as well as from neighboring peoples, the Ankole, the Toro, and the Bunyoro. The area around Lake Nyasa seems to have been one of the greatest sources of supply for the southern area. The principal victims were the Makua, Ngindo, and Nyanja. Others victims along the Ruvuma River were the Ajawa, the Madonda, and the Makonde.[13]

During the time the Arab slave dealers were on the coast or in Zanzibar, the local atmosphere was one of hostility and fear. Parents and relatives kept close watch over children, and few people, young or old, stirred at night because of the many instances of kidnaping, especially in and around the towns. There were several reports that Arabs actually raided African homes and captured the residents. These acts posed a serious threat to the sultan of Zanzibar, who hesitated to take any firm action against them because he feared reprisals from his Arab subjects, many of whom were directly engaged in the trade. He was also concerned about his prestige in Oman, where he still had family and friends. However, the fact that he received revenue from the trade was perhaps the most important reason why he tolerated it.[14]

For the most part, however, the coast was a base for interior raids. These activities were usually financed by Indian bankers. There were also a few Indians, mainly from Cutch, who participated directly in

IX, no. 1 (Spring, 1964), 220, 222; and H. Darley and N. A. Sharp, *Slave Trading and Slave Owning in Abyssinia* (London, 1922), p. 10.

13. Bombay, Political Department, May, 1860, sec. A, pp. 286–91; *ibid.*, June, 1869, pp. 248–49; Alison Smith, "The Southern Section of the Interior, 1840–84," in *East Africa*, ed. Oliver and Mathew, pp. 277, 286; and G. S. P. Freeman-Grenville, "The German Sphere, 1884–98," in *ibid.*, p. 433.

14. Bombay, Political Department, May, 1860, sec. A, pp. 286–91; and *ibid.*, June, 1869, pp. 248–49.

the trade. On several occasions British political and naval officers reported that banians (Hindu merchants) were buying and selling slaves and becoming wealthy in Zanzibar. There is no available evidence, however, that Indians actually organized and led slave caravans into the interior. Those who participated in the trade were bankers or dealers on the coast.[15]

Slave parties generally consisted of a few Arab dealers or their agents (usually Swahili), a small group of loyal armed guards, and some porters who carried supplies to exchange for slaves. As a rule the slave trade was well organized, although there were occasions when slavers raided indiscriminately, collected slaves, and organized convoys without the benefit of a slave market. On arriving at a village or market place, the Arab or Swahili head of the party would contact the local African ruler and promise him muskets, gunpowder, and other goods for slaves; sometimes the slavers encouraged war with a neighboring people for the purpose of capturing slaves. In the course of such wars, men, women, and children were carried away as villages burned. After a raid, other Africans were rounded up and organized in gangs for the march. Frequently, those first captured were not taken directly to the coast but were marched to other areas until a caravan large enough to send back was assembled.[16]

Although most slaves seem to have been taken either during or immediately after raids, there were other means of capture. When famine occurred, either because of adverse weather conditions or because slave raids destroyed crops and took away the necessary labor force, families sometimes sold their children, and individuals sometimes gave themselves into slavery. This was reasoned to be the best guarantee available of food and security. Another means of acquiring slaves was to spread food on the ground and catch hungry children who attempted to eat it. Kidnaping occurred in the interior as well as on the coast. But these means of capture provided only a small portion of the over-all trade.[17]

15. Bombay, Political Department, December 2, 1853, pp. 98–100; and *ibid.*, January, 1870, sec. A, pp. 4–45. This is discussed in greater detail on pp. 62–64 below.

16. Russell, *General Rigby*, pp. 128–31.

17. See Appendix 1.

Another means of obtaining slaves was from stations or contacts in the interior. In the eastern Sudan, for example, Arab merchants had agents who served as collectors or purchasers of slaves in the following towns: Shendi, Khartoum, Sennar, Gallabat, Kassala, and El Obeid. Shendi was a crossroads for most of the eastern Sudan trade:

> Here in the dusty, crowded market [are] rich Arab merchants from Suakin with cambric from Madras and coarse muslin from Bengal, with spices — cloves and ginger — and with sandal wood to exchange for gold brought down from Ethiopia, for slaves and for the spirited Dongola horses. . . . Four or five times a year caravans came from Kordofan and Darfur, bringing slaves from the Negro countries to the south. . . . From Sennar caravans arrive more frequently, . . . inevitably with slaves from Ethiopia — Galla women were in great demand.[18]

The following is an account of a similar slave market in Tanzania:

> The Swahili or Arab traders would send a message to Mfumwa Kengia informing him when they intended to arrive at his court. Then Kengia would make this news known to as large an area of North Pare as possible. On the appointed day, people who had slaves to dispose of brought them to Kiriche and tied them to a tree at the slave market. The traders came to the market and bargained for the prices.[19]

Until the middle of the nineteenth century, interior slave caravans frequently consisted of local people: the Bisa, who resided west of Lake Tanganyika; the Yao, who lived east of Lake Nyasa; and the Nyamwezi, who were to the north of Lake Nyasa. Farther north, the Kamba of present-day Kenya played an important role. In the second and third decades of the nineteenth century there was competition deep in the interior from the Arabs, the Swahili, the Portuguese, and their mulattoes. Later, from about 1870 to 1880, the interior trade routes were dominated by two powerful figures: Nyamwezi King Mirambo and the Swahili ruler Tippu Tib. Mirambo was successful in curtailing the Arab influence in the area between Tabora

18. Robin Hallett, *The Penetration of Africa* (New York, 1965), pp. 372–73.
19. Isaria Kimambo, *A Political History of the Pare* (Nairobi, 1969), p. 128.

and Lake Tanganyika, where he dominated the routes to Karagwe and Buganda. Tippu Tib, who sold ivory and slaves collected in the Congo region, was the most powerful man in the area just prior to the establishment of European hegemony. Chief Mlozi dominated the slave trade in the Lake Nyasa region. These new traders, supplied with Arab arms, expanded their activities deeper into the interior in response to an increased demand on the coast for ivory and slaves.

March to the Coast

The slaves' march to the coast was probably the most inhumane aspect of the entire operation. Women and children were normally bound with thongs, while men were usually harnessed in heavy two-pronged, Y-shaped sticks, bolted around the neck. To prevent escape at night, the handles of the forked sticks were tied together upright, thereby forcing the slaves to sleep with the bolt under their necks. In other cases, iron rings and chains were used to bind the slaves together on the march. The forked sticks or chains were kept on until the slave was delivered to the coast, which sometimes took several months.[20] Ignacius Pallme, a Bohemian traveler in Kordofan, described the procedure:

> As soon as they [slavers] have collected from three to six hundred, or perhaps a thousand slaves, the convoy is sent with an escort . . . to Lobeid. . . . A Sheba is hung around the neck of the full-grown slaves; it consists of a young tree about six or eight feet in length, and two inches in thickness, forming a fork in front; this is bound round the neck of the victim so that the stem of the tree presents anteriorly, the fork is closed at the back of the neck by a cross-bar, and fastened . . . by straps cut from raw hide; . . . the man in front takes the log of his successor . . . and this measure is repeated in succession. . . . The poor Negroes were driven on like cattle, but treated with far less care or forbearance.[21]

David Livingstone also recorded the inhumanity of this phase of the trade:

20. Bombay, Secret Department, May 17, 1843, p. 14.
21. Ignacius Pallme, *Travels in Kordofan* (London, 1834), p. 314.

We passed a woman tied by the neck to a tree, and dead. The people of the country explained that she had been unable to keep up with the other slaves in the gang, and her master had determined that she should not become the property of any one else if she recovered after resting for a time. I may mention here that we saw others tied up in a similar manner, and one lying in the path shot or stabbed, for she was in a pool of blood. The explanation we got invariably was that the Arab who owned these victims was enraged at losing his money by the slaves becoming unable to march, and vented his spleen by murdering them.[22]

Livingstone believed this was also to demonstrate to the other slaves the consequences of not completing the march. Livingstone noted:

We never realized the atrocious nature of the traffic until we saw it at the fountain-head. . . . Besides those actually captured, thousands are killed and die of their wounds and famine, driven from their villages by the slave raid proper.[23]

Slaves from the Bahr el Ghazal marched across several Ethiopian routes: through Karora on the northern route across the Blue Nile; across Shoa to the southern Red Sea and the Gulf of Aden ports; north of Shoa to the chief towns in Danakil country, branching off to the ports of Roheita or Beilul; through Entoto to Zeila; through Tigre to Massawa; and through Harar to Zeila, branching off and going to Jibuti or around the Gulf of Tajura. Marching time depended, of course, on conditions and points of origin, but estimates were, from the interior of Ethiopia: to Tajura, twenty-one days; to Roheita, twenty-seven days; to Beilul, twenty-one days. Tolls were paid per head to each chief through whose territory the slaves passed. From the Galla region to Massawa, for example, there were four tolls. This practice was a lucrative one for some kings; the king of Tajura reportedly derived most of his revenue from tolls and the trade generally.[24]

In 1873 British Consul John Kirk in Zanzibar had his vice-consul, Frederic Elton, investigate the extent of the slave traffic along the

22. David Livingstone, *The Last Journals of David Livingstone*, ed. Horace Waller (New York, 1875), p. 59.

23. *Ibid.*, p. 413.

24. Bombay, Secret Department, August 16, 1841, pp. 19–20.

coast. After extensive field trips, Elton found that in thirty days "no less than 4,096 slaves" marched north from Tanganyika. The Holmwood Report of 1874 and subsequent reports confirmed that the traffic was extensive. Kirk observed that the Treaty of 1873 between Zanzibar and Britain, which prohibited the sea trade in slaves, had stimulated a rise in trade on the overland routes. He noted that slaves were marched in chain gangs along the coast through Dar es Salaam as far as Lamu, and a few as far as Somali country. From Kilwa the march could have been as long as 700 miles. Arab informers reported that mainland slaves were also marched long distances to the south of Mafia Island in order to supply the demand of the French Indian Ocean colonies.[25]

In December, 1873, Elton described slaves chained in gangs of sixteen:

> One gang of lads and women, chained together with iron neck rings, was in a horrible state, their lower extremities coated with dry mud and their own excrement, and torn with thorns, their own bodies mere frameworks, and their skeleton limbs tightly stretched over with wrinkled, parchment-like skin.[26]

Four hundred of these slaves were being marched from the Lake Nyasa region to Kilwa, to be delivered to Sadani, Pangani, Wasseen, and Mombasa. Elton reported again on January 8, 1874:

> Whilst [I was] lying ill under a shed at Kikunia, on December thirtieth, a caravan of four hundred slaves passed through the village; and on the next day a far larger one (we counted 1000, and then stopped) of some 1,100 filed past within sight of my bed, in long chain gangs.[27]

A caravan leader, Mamji Hadh, said he

> had been away two years, did not know exactly how many slaves he had, more than one thousand certainly; was obliged to march slowly, as some had been a year and a half in the gangs.[28]

25. India, Political Department, September, 1878, sec. A, pp. 13–24.
26. Quoted in Edward Hutchinson, *The Slave Trade of East Africa* (London, 1874), p. 59.
27. *Ibid.*, p. 61.   28. *Ibid.*, p. 62.

He thought it good that the sea route was closed, because he saved the customs duty levied on each slave. He was bound for Pangani, where the customs master had advanced him all the provisions for the slave hunt and would control the selling.[29]

Again in 1874 Elton reported that he was shown a place set aside as a camping ground, where huts were built for wet weather, cooking trenches constructed, and spare logs and gang irons kept ready for slaves. He was told by one of the dealers:

> There has never been such a good year . . . ; we have fixed halting places, and send men ahead; everything is ready for us when we arrive.[30]

Continuing his investigations when he became consul at Portuguese Mozambique, Elton traveled up and down the coast and into the interior, compiling voluminous reports on the slave trade for the foreign office. His first journey was along the northern coast of Mozambique. He found hardly a village intact; the Makua inhabitants had been sold or had fled farther into the interior. A year later, on a trip south along the coast, Elton found the chief of the Makua dealing in slaves under an agreement with Swahili dealers.[31]

Elton's successor at Mozambique, Henry O'Neill, was also a diligent reporter on the slave trade. He described caravans along the Ruvuma River, where Matamba was the southern entrepôt. Most of the slaves were Ajawa, Madonda, and Makonde, who were forced to carry ivory and tobacco to the coast. O'Neill reported that two routes from the Lake Nyasa region led to the Mozambique coast, one at Ibo and the other at Quelimane.[32]

Shortly after the Treaty of 1873, an ivory and slave merchant reported:

> The Government, by preventing the transportation of slaves by way of the rivers, has only increased the evil. I will tell you why. When

29. *Ibid.*, p. 61.

30. *Ibid.*

31. Great Britain, Foreign Office, Vol. 84 (*Slave Trade*, Vol. 1411), Elton to F.O., June 21, 1875.

32. *Ibid.* (Vol. 1565), O'Neill to F.O., July 3, 1880, Encl. no. 1; *ibid.*, O'Neill to F.O., December 3, 1880, Encl., no. 1; and *ibid.* (Vol. 1616), O'Neill to F.O., January 12, 1882.

the transport was made with boats, although the slaves were heaped together in great quantity, the mortality only reached ten percent. But now that this route is hindered, what happens? Bands of thousands of Arabs gather in Kordofan, and descend to devastate the country. The slaves were made to walk over mountains, through woods and across deserts for months and months before arriving at Kordofan, and during the journey water and grain became scarce, and only a third part of the caravan reaches its destination.[33]

The caravan routes were often covered with the sick, the dying, and the dead. Much of this resulted from the brutality of the slavers and their assistants; but some was due to an insufficient supply of food and water. Capt. W. C. Harris observed in 1843 that slaves received a daily ration of four handfuls of parched grain — a mixture of wheat and maize. No meat was provided. Slaves in other caravans no doubt fared even worse. Christopher Rigby reported that on one short march 125 of 600 slaves expired on the road. A shortage of food and a lack of medical care seem to have been responsible for that high mortality rate. Seldom was the mortality rate less than 20 per cent.[34]

Coastal Markets

The slave markets were scattered along the East African coast, from northern Somali, around Cape Guardafui, and along the southern coast including the following towns: Merca, Mogadishu, Brava, Lamu, Malindi, Mombasa, Pangani, Bagamoyo, Dar es Salaam, Ibo, Moçambique, Quelimane, Sofala, and the islands of Pemba, Zanzibar, and Madagascar. The focal point, however, was the island of Zanzibar, which lies about twenty-four miles off the coast of present-day Tanzania. This was a very suitable location for the slave depot; it was close enough to the mainland to serve as a base for raids up and down the coast but was surrounded by a natural moat wide enough to protect against African or European interference from the mainland. In addition, the island is in the direct line of the monsoons,

33. Romolo Gessi Pasha, *Seven Years in the Sudan* (London, 1892), pp. 334–35.

34. Bombay, Secret Department, May 17, 1843, p. 14; and Russell, *General Rigby*, pp. 128–31.

19

which were of use to the Arab dhows as well as to American and European clipper ships in sailing to and from the East African coast.

The port of Kilwa, which lies about 150 miles south of Zanzibar, became a principal emporium at which thousands of slaves were collected for sale and export. Many, possibly most, of the slaves sold at the Kilwa market were exported to Zanzibar. They were packed in open boats and exposed to the weather; often the supply of food and water was inadequate. The journey to Zanzibar usually took from one to three days, but inclement weather could extend the voyage to as long as ten days, with a resultant heavy loss of life. Capt. Fairfax Moresby, for example, reported a case in which fewer than a dozen slaves out of three hundred survived a ten-day voyage. The slaves who reached Zanzibar usually were suffering from starvation. Since a duty was charged for each slave passing through customs, the sick often were not considered worth the duty and were left to die. Rigby has described the landings of slaves at Zanzibar:

> They are frequently in the last stage of lingering starvation and unable to stand. Some drop dead in the custom-house and in the streets. Others who are not likely to recover are left on board to die in order that the owner may avoid paying the duty which is levied on those landed. After being brought on shore the slaves are kept some time in the dealers' houses until they gain strength and flesh when they are taken to the slave market and sold to the highest bidder.[35]

It seems that most slaves were placed on sale in the open market, but in some cases slave buyers overseas wrote letters to dealers in Zanzibar requesting slaves. Nine such letters written in Arabic and captured by the British consul at Zanzibar were orders from Omani Arabs for supplies of slaves. On further investigation, the British political agent in Muscat learned that such orders were normal and that deliveries were usually made at predetermined places on the Arabian coast.[36]

According to Elton, the sultan announced the opening of trade in the open market in an official proclamation, which he affixed to the door of the customs house. Elton described the market:

35. Quoted in Russell, *General Rigby*, p. 333.

36. Bombay, Political Department, February, 1862, sec. A, pp. 31–36; and India, Secret Department, March, 1889, sec. E, pp. 98–106.

Lanes of natives — men, women and children, squalid and spare from travelling, exposure and semi-starvation are sitting on the ground, separated in batches according to their estimated value and quality. . . . This is the Slave Market, open every afternoon from five until sun-down for the transaction of business.[37]

Some of the slaves

are mere skeletons of skin and bones, festering with sores and loathsome skin-diseases, and looking as if they were on the very threshold of death. . . . The mouth is opened, the teeth examined, the eyes carefully looked at, the hands and nails passed muster; the limbs handled, and the condition felt in exactly the same manner in which a horse would be looked over at a fair; and when the competition is eager, and the lot is passed over from one intending buyer to another, each one stepping aside to put one or two questions and endeavoring to ascertain temper — an important qualification — and finally, in the case of women, retiring with the chattel under the cover of an adjacent shed, the more minutely to estimate the value of her attractions — one turns away with a feeling of sickness and disgust at such an exhibition being possible in this civilized age. . . . My picture is far from being overdrawn.[38]

Rigby quoted a contemporary account:

The market [Zanzibar] was well on when we arrived. There were perhaps twenty auctioneers, each attending a separate group and selling away as hard as possible. One of the officers [British naval] counted over 300 slaves present. . . . The price of one boy was seven dollars; he was stripped and examined, his eyes looked at, and finally he was rejected.[39]

Another contemporary observer noted:

In another portion of the square are a number of women, forming several semi-circles. Their bodies are painted and their figures exposed. . . , with barely a yard of cloth around their hips. Rows of girls from the age of twelve and upwards are exposed to the examina-

37. Quoted in E. A. Loftus, *Elton and the East African Coast Slave Trade* (London, 1952), pp. 5, 6.

38. *Ibid.*, pp. 8–9.

39. Quoted in Russell, *General Rigby*, p. 213.

tions of throngs of Arabs and subjected to inexpressible indignities by the brutal dealers.[40]

The Zanzibar slave mart was obviously filthy. Its area was about 400 square feet. On one side was a fort to guard the business, and on the other side were houses for the market employees. There was an auctioneer for each group of slaves, who were displayed in rows, males and females separately. For the actual auctioning, the slaves were generally clothed and neat. The women wore necklaces, bracelets, and anklets, all of which the dealer retained after the sale and used for other slave women. Prices varied, depending on the supply and the time of year; the highest prices were paid between December and March, when many Arab buyers were in the market. Zanzibar and Kilwa commanded the best prices, because the sultan rather rigidly controlled the markets as well as the import-export duties, from which he received commissions. In addition to foreign currency, which was used primarily on the coast, cloth, jewelry, dates, and firearms were widely used in exchange for slaves. It has been estimated that about three-quarters of the slaves annually imported into Zanzibar were re-exported, and these figures do not, of course, include those smuggled in or out to avoid paying customs.[41]

With regard to the Abyssinian markets, Henry Salt, in 1814, said that slaves, ivory, and gold (in that order) were the only significant exports of the country. Some forty years later, in October, 1858, Brigadier Coghlan observed that while cattle and foodstuffs were exported from Tajura, Massawa, and Zeila, the slave traffic was the most lucrative. Thirty-two years later, after the trade was supposedly abolished, the political agent at Aden, Colonel Stace, reported that the slave trade from the southern part of the Red Sea and the Gulf of Tajura had increased "enormously of late."[42]

In the 1870s the Red Sea ports became the principal points of slave

40. Quoted in G. L. Sulivan, *Dhow Chasing in Zanzibar Waters* (London, 1873), pp. 253–54.

41. Bombay, Secret Department, November 4, 1843, p. 9; and *idem.*, Political Department, June, 1869, sec. A, pp. 248–49.

42. Henry Salt, *A Voyage to Abyssinia* (London, 1814), pp. 383–84, 425–26; India, External Department, June, 1886, sec. A, pp. 155–58; and *idem*, Secret Department, August, 1890, pp. 310–12.

embarkation for the East. When Egypt and Britain signed an agreement in 1877 to abolish the slave trade within seven years, the Nile Valley trade into Egypt was increasingly restricted. This resulted in a proportionate increase in the number of slaves from the northeastern Sudan and Ethiopia who were channeled to the Red Sea ports. At this time the agreement between Zanzibar and Britain to abolish the slave trade was restricting the trade in the Zanzibar region. Some reports hold that by 1876 the annual flow of slaves in the Red Sea ports numbered about 30,000, many of whom were shipped to southern Arabia and the Persian Gulf region.[43]

The slave trade was big business; except for low customs duties, the selling price was often clear profit, especially in cases where the slaves had been kidnaped or captured in raids, as was the most common practice. But even when purchased in the interior, a slave normally cost only a few yards of cheap cloth. Hundreds of slaves were exchanged for a few weapons and ammunition, not to mention mere trinkets. And there was little cost for the upkeep of the caravan. The crew lived mostly off the land, raiding farms, gathering wild foods, and hunting. There were no lodging costs; everyone normally slept in the open, except in a few cases where the caravan leaders slept in tents. Transportation costs were minimal; slave porters were used to take the merchandise and some amenities into the interior; on the return to the coast slaves frequently were forced to carry ivory and tobacco, which were sold along with themselves. There were a few Swahili assistants to the caravan leaders, but, unfortunately, there seems to be no information about their fees; however, even if they were paid, this could not have greatly offset the high profits that, for the most part, went to the Arab slave dealers and Indian bankers.

The African Involvement

The development of the slave trade obviously occurred with the complicity of some Africans. The paramount cause of the slave trade, however, was the demand of Arabs and Europeans who were deter-

43. Pasha, *Seven Years in the Sudan*, pp. 221, 331; and Gray, *Southern Sudan*, p. 182.

mined to initiate and maintain the trade with or without African assistance. This is clear from the fact that kidnapings characterized the
early stages of the traffic and remained a practice throughout the
slave-trading period, even though the African-assisted raids became
the main source of supply.

African allies were frequently mulattoes, either African and Arab
or African and European. They were part of two communities: they
spoke the language and practiced the customs of both and had stakes
in both. However, the stronger attraction was often the economic
gain to be derived from cooperating with the Arab or European slave
dealers. Thus, many mulattoes employed their knowledge of African
languages and customs to raid African villages for economic gain.

Not only did Arab and European slavers exploit conflicts between
Africans in order to win allies, but they also convinced Africans that
their participation in the slave trade would result in political and
economic gains. Thus some Africans, like native participants on other
continents at other times, succumbed to the desire for wealth and
power. In East Africa the Yao of northern Mozambique, the Nyamwezi of Tanzania, the Baganda of Uganda, and others were important
merchants in the interior prior to European or Arab penetration.
Long-distance trade was well established with metal tools and ivory
as the principal products. Indeed, during the period of the slave trade,
ivory was only rarely replaced by the slave as an important item in
trade. African merchants, therefore, were well entrenched in legitimate trade and were determined to maintain their hegemony, even
when that required involvement in the slave trade.

Political rulers also saw certain practical advantages to participation in the trade. For Kengia of North Pare, for example:

> The slave market at Kiriche may have convinced him further that a
> strong control over the trade would increase his political power and
> probably make him the strongest ruler in North Pare.[44]

The crucial factor which encouraged African political leaders and
merchants to participate in the slave trade was the introduction of
firearms. Those who acquired firearms could solidify their position

44. Kimambo, *History of the Pare*, p. 130.

in society, conquer new territory, and dominate other people and economies; the price of firearms was a supply of labor in the form of African captives.

In time this state of affairs, in which one's economic and political power or status came to rest to such a great extent on a trade in men, caused the inner fabric of some African societies to degenerate: where criminal liability and punishment in early African societies did not normally include enslavement, during the peak of the slave trade individuals were enslaved for crimes and for violating traditional taboos.

These are some of the reasons why Africans participated in the Arab- and European-initiated slave trade, reasons that led to the perversion of certain values in African societies. When the slave trade was terminated, Africans were condemned by Europeans as barbarians who lived in a state of anarchy and tribal warfare. To whatever extent that may have been true, and many Africans could not justly be so characterized, European and Arab slave-trading activities were major contributors to that state of affairs.

2.

The Sea Voyage, Slave Marts, and Dispersion in Asia

ARAB MERCHANTS sailed from Arabia and the Persian Gulf region from November to March during the northeastern monsoon, did business along the East African coast and in Zanzibar, where they purchased or kidnaped slaves, and began their return to Asian markets with the southwestern monsoon in April. Most of these merchants had left East Africa by the beginning of June because the monsoon winds reached their greatest intensity between June and August. But those few who did not manage to leave before June — for a variety of reasons, including their failure to obtain as many slaves as they wanted — returned to Asian ports in September or October when the monsoon winds were calmer.[1]

Among the several African ports of embarkation in the north were Tajura, Roheita, and Beilul. Those slaves who embarked at Tajura were normally taken through the broad Bab el Mandeb Strait and then across to the coast at Mocha, where they were landed. Some of the slaves were then marched or reshipped to Mocha, Hodeida, or Jedda, where they were sold.[2] Embarkation at Roheita usually began at night so that the coast near Mocha could be reached by dawn the next morning. From Mocha, the dhows sailed north, making use of the several reefs for water supplies and, during the nineteenth century, seeking

1. Bombay, External Department, May, 1855, sec. A, "Report on the Slave Trade in the Persian Gulf," pp. 131–41.

2. India, Secret Department, August 16, 1889, "Annual Report on the Slave Trade for 1888," pp. 68–80.

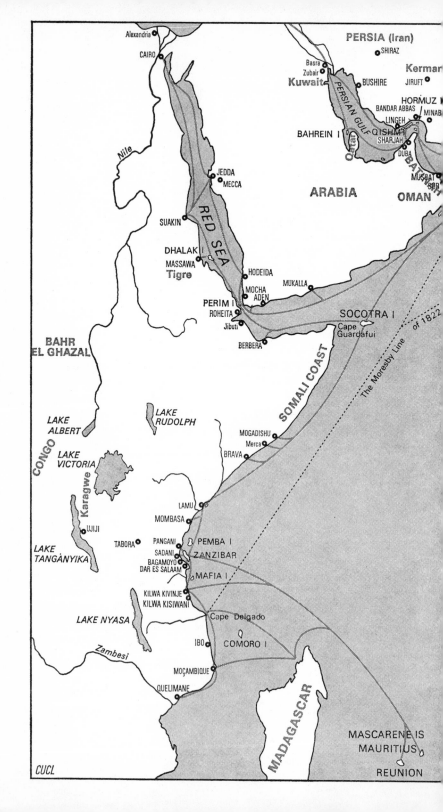

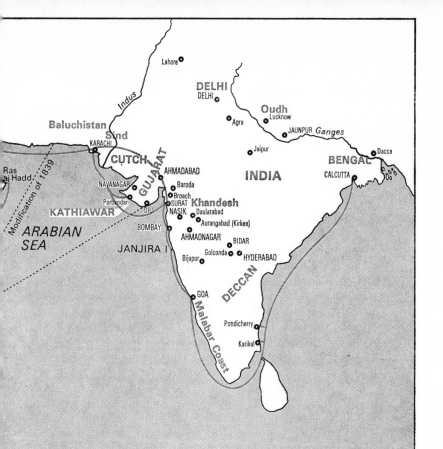

Map 2. Scope of the East African Slave Trade

0   1000   ━━━━━━ Trade Routes

Miles

cover from British cruisers attempting to suppress the traffic. Those slaves destined for Hodeida were debarked on the outskirts and were marched into the city in small groups because Hodeida was well patrolled by the Turkish authorities, who frequently seized slave cargoes and confiscated the dhows. The seized slaves were often sold then by the Turks.[3] From Beilul, slave dhows destined for Jedda sailed north, inside the reefs on the east side of the Red Sea, and sought news of British cruisers and authorities. British naval officers estimated that the crossing from Beilul to Jedda and from Roheita to Jedda took nine and fourteen hours, respectively. Dhows from Beilul and Roheita were often owned by dealers in Jedda and manned by Arabs from the Red Sea area. Most of the dhows were described by British commanders as well manned and armed.[4]

A great Arab slave-trading family in Aden, the Abu Bakr, kept watch for its slavers and had a telegraph system to maintain contact with several entrepôts. In some cases, news was telegraphed from Aden to Bab el Mandeb Strait, through which dhows frequently passed. Messengers were sent to Tajura from the island of Perim, or telegraph signals were relayed to Assab, where a line probably connected with Beilul. Another warning system existed at Ras al Hadd, the most easterly point of Arabia, where the villagers watched for British cruisers and signaled slavers or their agents.[5]

To the south, Zanzibar was the main port for slave shipments to Asia. Slaves shipped from the East African mainland ports of Pangani and Bagamoyo normally arrived in Zanzibar within a few hours. Other slaves were brought to Zanzibar from farther south. Swahili dhows sailed along the northwest coast of Madagascar collecting slaves, who were taken to depots in Mozambique. Later these slaves were taken to Ibo and Kilwa Kisiwani; from there it took about three days to sail to Zanzibar if the weather was favorable.[6]

3. *Ibid.*

4. *Ibid.*

5. *Ibid.*

6. Great Britain, Foreign Office, Vol. 84 (*Slave Trade*, Vol. 1078), Cape Commissioners to F.O., January 23, 1859; Reginald Coupland, *East Africa and Its Invaders* (Oxford, 1938), p. 230; and Charles E. B. Russell, *General Rigby, Zanzibar and the Slave Trade* (London, 1935), p. 134.

The trip from Zanzibar via Lamu to the Red Sea, took about ten days in good weather; from Zanzibar to Muscat, about thirty days, including normal stops for food and water. Because of the increased restrictions on the slave trade during the nineteenth century, the dhows were careful to avoid British cruisers. They made most of their trips at night and almost always hugged the shore as they moved northward, making use of the inlets and reefs up to Lamu or Brava, from which they usually sailed for the Red Sea or the Gulf of Oman ports. It was therefore easy for the slavers to rush to the shore and dispose of their cargo if a British cruiser were spotted. In many cases, the cruisers could not get close to the shore because of sand bars and rocks. This, together with the speed of the dhows, minimized the likelihood of capture by the British navy. Also the number of cruisers on patrol was always small, and abolition efforts were largely ineffective.[7]

The average dhow was fifty feet long (length on deck), fifteen feet wide (beam), and eight feet deep (depth of hold). Capt. P. Colomb, who commanded a British cruiser from 1862 to 1870, observed that a dhow of 80 to 100 tons could carry 100 to 150 slaves to the Persian Gulf. Some of the dhows were fitted with a long beam along the bottom of the boat to which the slaves' ankles were attached with iron anklets.[8] The dhow captain was usually Arab, but his crew frequently included Africans, some of whom were hired slaves secured from a master to whom they were returned after a voyage or season. All of the African crew were quasi-free in that they were not for sale, could manage their own funds, and could travel "freely" with the captain. In some instances, however, slave crews were purchased in Africa and sold for large profits in Arabia or the Persian Gulf.[9]

7. Bombay, Political Department, May, 1860, sec. A, pp. 286–91; India, External Department, January, 1887, sec. A, p. 26; *idem*, Political Department, November, 1880, sec. A, pp. 58–64; and Reginald Coupland, *The Exploitation of East Africa, 1856–1890: The Slave Trade and the Scramble* (1939; reprint ed., Evanston, Ill., 1967), p. 154.

8. Bombay, Political Department, June, 1869, pp. 248–49; India, Secret Department, August, 1889, sec. E, pp. 68–80; and P. Colomb, *Slave Catching in the Indian Ocean* (London, 1873), pp. 48–49.

9. India, External Department, March, 1885, sec. A, pp. 1–23; and Bombay, Political Department, June, 1869, pp. 248–49.

The best description of the actual voyages are those provided by contemporary observers. Captain Moresby, for example, observed:

> The Negroes are then stowed, in the literal sense of the word, in bulk, the first along the floor of the vessel, two adults side by side, with a boy or girl resting between or on them, until the tier is complete. Over them the first platform is laid, supported an inch or two clear of their bodies, where a second tier is stowed, and so on until they reach above the gunwale of the vessel. . . . Those of the lower portion of the cargo that die cannot be removed. They remain until the upper part are dead and thrown over.[10]

Capt. G. L. Sulivan, who served on three ships that patrolled the Indian Ocean between 1849 and 1868 to help enforce suppression, described a dhow caught on the Somali coast:

> Twenty-three women huddled together, one or two with infants in their arms. These women were literally doubled up, there being no room to sit erect. On a bamboo deck, about three feet above the keel, were forty-eight men, crowded together in the same way; and on another deck above this were fifty-three children. Some of the slaves were in the last stages of starvation and dysentery.[11]

Another observer noted:

> The sea passage exposes the slave to much suffering; and, in addition to the danger from overcrowding and insufficient food and water, the loss of life connected with the attempt to escape His Majesty's cruisers is very considerable, it being the practice to use any means to get rid of the slaves in order to escape condemnation should the dhow be captured.[12]

An Egyptian steamer in the Red Sea captured two vessels containing 850 slaves between them, a large number even for steamers in the East African trade. The slaves were

10. Quoted in Reginald Coupland, *The Anti-Slavery Movement* (London, 1933), p. 197. See also *idem, Exploitation of East Africa*, p. 141; and G. L. Sulivan, *Dhow Chasing in Zanzibar Waters* (London, 1873), p. 110.

11. Sulivan, *Dhow Chasing*, pp. 168–69.

12. Edward Hutchinson, *The Slave Trade of East Africa* (London, 1874), p. 38.

packed together like anchovies, the living and the dying festering together, and the dead lying beneath them. . . . The slaves were in a state of starvation, having had nothing to eat for several days.[13]

The very limited documentation of the sea voyage from Zanzibar to Asia results, no doubt, from the fact that the Arab dealers and crews did not keep many records of the slave trade, certainly not on the more inhumane aspects of it. The numerous accounts about the march from the African interior were written by foreigners, mainly European explorers, missionaries, and officials, all of whom investigated the traffic; but those observers did not accompany the cargoes to Asia. The few accounts available are those given by captains of British cruisers attempting to suppress the trade, and their usual concern was to determine if a ship was carrying slaves and, if so, to free them. The dhows were small compared with European vessels and did not generally carry passengers, as did the few Turkish and Egyptian steamers in the Red Sea.

The scarcity of records by observers is supplemented, however, by a few statements of liberated Africans.[14] Some of those statements indicate the number of slaves on board a given dhow, and some mention that many died during the sea voyage, but scarcely any other details are given about the voyage. This could mean that it was not a catastrophic ordeal, that the memory of it was blurred by time and subsequent treatment, or that the European's questions unconsciously steered the former slave's answers away from the worst aspects of the voyage. In any event, the scarcity of slave statements on this vital aspect of the traffic is most unfortunate. Perhaps continued research will reveal more information.

The data presently available presents a very grim picture. The slaves were crowded in the dhows. Moreover, the supply of water and food (usually fish and rice) was often inadequate even for the crew, who sometimes became ill. Undernourishment and starvation were not uncommon aspects of the sea voyage to Asia. Mutinies on dhows do not seem to have been numerous, but the way in which the slaves were packed, along with the positioning of the crew in higher positions

13. Sir Samuel Baker, *The Albert N'Yanza* (New York, 1962), II, 538.
14. See Appendix 1.

where they could readily respond to attempted rebellion, minimized the number of opportunities for slave resistance during the voyage.[15]

Shipments to India

There is very little evidence that many slaves were shipped directly from East Africa to India, although some were sent to the present-day areas of Pakistan and India's northwestern coast of Gujarat. In 1835, for example, the superintendent of the Indian navy reported that an average of five boats per year sailed from Porbandar with produce for Africa and returned with slaves. He also reported a regular slave traffic on a small scale between Mozambique and Diu.[16] But documentation is inadequate to conclude that there was any major overseas slave traffic between East Africa and India. By far the greatest number of African slaves and freedmen to enter India seem to have come from Arabia and the Persian Gulf via Sind, Cutch, and Kathiawar to Baroda, Broach, Surat, Bombay, and other points on the west coast of India.

There is evidence that Ethiopian kings, seeking to establish good relations with their Asian counterparts, especially the Mughuls, sent them numerous goods and slaves. The seventeenth-century traveler and chronicler, François Bernier, has recorded that an Ethiopian king dispatched to the Great Mughul twelve horses, a mule, two elephant's teeth, and twenty-five slaves. An Armenian Christian and a Muslim, both merchants from Ethiopia, were to deliver the gifts. To cover their expenses and provide a commission, the merchants received from the king an additional thirty-two slaves, who were sold in Mocha.[17] The group arrived at the port of Surat in Gujarat and then marched inland to the court of the Muslim sovereign, Aurangzib, who received the presents (only seven or eight of the slaves seem to have survived) and in exchange paid the emissaries. To the Ethiopian

15. India, Secret Department, August, 1889, sec. E, pp. 68–80; and Bombay, Secret Department, October 12, 1842, pp. 17–26. See also Appendix 1.

16. Bombay, Political Department, September 19, 1836, pp. 10, 11.

17. François Bernier, *Travels in the Moghul Empire, 1656–1668* (London, 1916) ; and *idem*, "Travels in the Moghul Empire," in *A General Collection of the Best and Most Interesting Voyages and Travels in All Parts of the World*, ed. John Pinkerton (London, 1811), pp. 133–44.

king, Aurangzib sent a vest, two silver and gilt trumpets, two silver timbals, a dagger covered with jewels, and gold and silver coins. In addition, he donated money to rebuild an old Ethiopian mosque which was the tomb of a great Muslim who had left Mecca to propagate Islam in Ethiopia.[18]

Other accounts like Bernier's suggest that commercial, and thus political and social, relations between Africans and Indians were developed and maintained successfully without the intercession of Arabs or Europeans. It is also clear that at least some African sovereigns voluntarily sent slaves as gifts to Asian kings. How many Africans reached any part of Asia in this manner can hardly be ascertained, but several travel accounts given by Europeans and Arabs during the Middle Ages very likely contain valuable information which could make a substantial contribution to the clarification of this problem.

There long existed a considerable importation into Calcutta of African slaves by Arab merchants from the Red Sea area. According to one early-nineteenth-century report, from ten to thirty Africans frequently arrived by ship. These slaves consisted of adults and children of both sexes, but females were most numerous; of the males, many were eunuchs. Most were already Muslims. Some of them were purchased by residents of Calcutta, but most were carried to Lucknow and other places in the interior. Most of the slaves were purchased to serve as domestic servants. The price in Calcutta fluctuated, but African eunuchs were usually sold for twice as much as ordinary males. African women were normally even more expensive. By comparison, Hindu and Muslim Arab boys and girls from Dacca and the surrounding area were sold as domestics for about one-tenth as much as a comparable African.[19]

Slave Marts
and Dispersion in Asia

As we have seen, the principal slave markets on the African side of the Red Sea and the Gulf of Aden were Suakin, Massawa, Roheita,

18. Bernier, "Travels," pp. 133–44.

19. *Irish University Press Series of British Parliamentary Papers* (Shannon, 1969), *Slave Trade,* LXXXVIII, 16–17.

Beilul, Tajura, and Zeila. The slave dhows sailing from these ports normally delivered their cargoes to the Arabian markets of Mocha, Hodeida, Jedda, and some smaller towns. Others went to the southern Arabian area around Mukalla. Most of the slave cargoes from the southern coast of East Africa, however, as well as some from the Red Sea ports, sailed for entrepôts such as Sharjah, Sur, Muscat, Bandar Abbas, Lingeh, Bahrein, Bushire, Kuwait, Basra, and a few others. From all of these ports of entry, slaves were marched to interior markets for sale. Although this was the general pattern, the distance of markets from the point of origin, the demand at a given time in a particular Asian area, and the extent to which British cruisers enforced restrictive measures were all important determinants of where slaves from any part of Africa were taken.

The season of greatest activity for the trade in the Red Sea area was during the Hadj, the pilgrimage to Mecca. This usually coincided with the southwestern monsoon, from April to October, which enabled dhows to make the trip northward from East Africa to Arabia. Slave brokers and their agents from various parts of the Muslim world gathered in several Arab cities and towns to conduct business with pilgrims who were returning from Mecca. These pilgrims frequently purchased one or two domestic slaves to take back with them.

The ports of Mocha, Hodeida, and Jedda were the chief slave marts on the Arabian side of the Red Sea in terms of both frequency of slave runs and over-all numbers imported. This was because the distance across the Red Sea was relatively short, and the British cruisers there were generally ineffective, mainly because of the protective Turkish and Egyptian influence which had long prevailed in the region. Another factor was that many pilgrims annually passed through these towns on their return from Mecca.

Mocha seems to have been the busiest port of entry, probably because it was located near the narrowest point on the Red Sea between Africa and Arabia and was also just opposite the major African entrepôts of Roheita, Tajura, and Zeila. From Mocha, slaves were reshipped or marched to Hodeida, Jedda, and other Arabian towns; sometimes they were shipped to Persian Gulf towns or, occasionally, as far as India. Most slaves destined for Hodeida or Jedda, however, were shipped there directly from Africa. Hodeida and Jedda, in addition to serving as markets for other Arabian towns, supplied Egypt, especially during the second half of the nineteenth century. Slaves were reported to be constantly on view in Jedda, though most of the actual sales were conducted in private homes. Prices varied, but women and girls, the great bulk of the trade, were the most expensive.[20]

In the Persian Gulf region, the busiest season for the slave trade coincided with the harvesting and marketing of dates, which were sold principally in Basra, Bandar Abbas, and along part of the Batinah coast. Harvesting began in July, and marketing continued into September. In many cases, slaves were exchanged for dates, which were traded in Africa for new supplies of slaves.

Lt. Col. A. D. Robertson, British resident in the Persian Gulf, estimated that, as early as 1828, between 1,400 and 1,700 slaves were imported directly into Muscat each year. This was a major distributing center on the Gulf of Oman, where profits were reported at about 20 to 25 per cent. Several observers noted that most households had two or three domestic African slaves, and frequently some were hired out for wages. Another active Omani port of entry and distributing center was Sur, which received cargoes of slaves by sea and overland routes.[21]

Dhows from Zanzibar also landed cargoes of slaves at Sharjah. Some of these slaves were then shipped to markets in nearby regions. Some slaves from Zanzibar were shipped as far as Bushire, where an estimated 50 per cent profit was not uncommon. Lingeh and Bahrein were important pearling centers, and slave pearl divers were in great demand. The British political agent at Bahrein, Capt. W. F. Prideaux, reported that pearl diving was so deleterious to health that middle-aged Africans were hard to find. Therefore divers were always

20. Bombay, Secret Department, August 16, 1841, pp. 19–20; *idem*, External Department, May, 1855, sec. A, pp. 131–41; *idem*, Political Department, April, 1871, sec. A, pp. 40–51; India, Political Department, October, 1877, sec. A, pp. 1–55; *ibid.*, July, 1883, sec. A, I, 14–25; Bombay, Political Department, March, 1865, sec. A, p. 297; India, Secret Department, October, 1895, sec. E, pp. 385–92; and *idem*, External Department, February, 1891, sec. A, pp. 172–73.

21. Bombay, Secret Department, October 12, 1842, pp. 17–26; *idem*, Political Department, January, 1870, sec.A, p. 296; India, External Department, February, 1891, sec. A, pp. 172–73; and Bombay, Political Department, February, 1862, sec. A, pp. 31–36.

in high demand. As late as the 1890s the Bahrein sheik, Zaid-ibn-Khalifa, told the political agent that the demand for slave pearl divers was great.[22]

Turkey and the areas north of the Persian Gulf were supplied with slaves by the markets in Bahrein, Lingeh, Kuwait, and Basra. Perhaps the largest of these entrepôts was Basra, where 50 per cent profits seem to have been normal. Boats unloaded at Basra and along the Euphrates River route to Baghdad, where profits were even higher. The consul general at Baghdad reported that 3,000 to 4,000 slaves were imported into Basra in 1861. Kuwait also had a considerable slave traffic, especially young girls destined for the northern region of the Persian Gulf. The Kuwaiti sheik himself was accused of direct involvement in the traffic. From Kuwait, slave parties were dispatched in small groups on land and sea to Zubair and to Basra, where brokers sold slaves in their homes. The surplus was marched along the Tigris and Euphrates rivers to Baghdad.[23]

Although Turkey historically received its greatest supply of African slaves from North Africa (Tripoli, Benghazi, and Alexandria), the increasing European control over the Mediterranean Sea during the nineteenth century caused a large portion of the Turkish demand to shift to the Red Sea area and to Baghdad. The British consul at Baghdad reported in 1842 that a lively trade in slaves was being carried on along the Euphrates River and that Turkish subjects conducted sales in Lingeh and Basra. Many of those slaves had reportedly been bought in the bazaars of Mecca and other Arabian cities. They

22. Bombay, Political Department, December 29, 1849, p. 35; *idem*, Secret Department, October 12, 1842, pp. 17–26; *idem*, Political Department, November 20, 1847, p. 43; India, Secret Department, August, 1896, sec. E, pp. 86–92; *ibid.*, December, 1905, sec. E, pp. 465–67; and *ibid.*, July, 1913, sec. G, pp. 16–41. Pearl diving was arduous and debilitating. A ship would normally sail with two teams of divers. One team descended with baskets into the water and pulled oysters from rocks and coral. When a diver's basket was full or when he could no longer remain in the water (his nose was clamped), the diver surfaced, unloaded his basket, and made another dive for a catch. Each slave made about ten dives before his team was replaced by the other one. The procedure continued all day, with breaks only when the boat changed location.

23. Bombay, Secret Department, October 12, 1842, pp. 17–27; *ibid.*, January 3, 1842, p. 58; *idem*, Political Department, August, 1861, sec. A, p. 225; *idem*, Secret Department, January 28, 1853, pp. 171–72; *idem*, Political Department, January 30, 1839, p. 31; and *ibid.*, August 8, 1838, p. 10.

arrived either in caravans from Basra and from Kuwaiti markets, as has been pointed out, or they came in boats, as passengers or servants of Muslims. The British political agent in Turkish Arabia wrote that many Iraqi homes, notably in Baghdad, had male and female African slaves of all ages. He also reported that vessels from Basra traded with India.[24]

Duties of the Slaves

The African slaves in Asia performed a variety of tasks. Some were used as pearl divers, mainly around Bahrein and Lingeh. Plantation slaves were most common on the Batinah coast, around Minab (inland from Bandar Abbas), and around Basra, where there were large date plantations which employed gang slave labor. A great number of male slaves seem to have been used as soldiers dating back to at least the seventh century, when some of them revolted in Mesopotamia.

In several areas, especially the Persian Gulf region, there was a preference for Habshis as domestic slaves.[25] Some Habshis were converted to Islam and were educated by their masters, eventually rising to trustworthy positions as stewards and supervisors of households and work forces. Others were hired out by their masters to work in small businesses, on dhows, and on farms and docks, and in many cases

---

24. Bombay, Secret Department, October 12, 1842, pp. 17–26; *ibid.*, February 25, 1848, pp. 27–28, 29–30; *idem*, Political Department, April, 1871, sec. A, pp. 40–51; and India, External Department, January, 1891, pp. 158–64.

25. *Habshi* (*Habashi, Hubshi, Hubshee*) and *Siddi* (*Siddhi, Seedee*) are terms commonly used to refer to Africans in Asian history. *Siddi* is allegedly derived from a corruption of *Sayyeed*, suggesting that it was not intended as a derogatory term. *Habshi* is said to be derived from the Arabic word *habash*, which means mixed, referring to persons in southern Arabia with both African and Arab ancestors. The Ethiopianist, Richard Pankhurst, holds that the term originally denoted a South Arabian people named Habashat, who settled on the African side of the Red Sea during the seventh century. There may be no contradiction between these two views. See Richard Pankhurst, *An Introduction to the Economic History of Ethiopia* (London, 1961), p. 55 n.

Habshi came to be used to refer to slaves from the Red Sea area, while *Siddi* applied to those slaves from the southern region. However, both terms are used in historical and contemporary literature and in present-day conversations in India and the Persian Gulf to refer generally to Asians of African descent. This is the way the terms will be used in this study, unless specifically indicated otherwise.

they were allowed to keep part of their earnings. Upper-class Arabs often owned eunuchs, who usually were well treated. A eunuch sometimes became his master's confidant.[26]

Most African females were domestic slaves. The greatest demand by affluent Arabs was for concubines, preferably Habshi girls protected by Habshi eunuchs. The reasons given for this choice were that Habshi girls were more beautiful than Siddi girls and that Habshi eunuchs were more loyal than Siddi eunuchs and knew the language of the girls. In any case, Habshis were generally treated better than Siddis and more frequently were regarded as members of the family. The Siddi domestic slaves performed the heavier household duties, such as preparing the meals, cleaning the quarters, running ordinary errands, and attending the gardens and the cattle. In general, the treatment of all domestic slaves was better than that of plantation and dock slaves.[27]

Some African male slaves were used as crew on dhows engaged in slave and legitimate commerce in the Red Sea, the Persian Gulf, and the Indian Ocean, while others were workers on the docks in those areas. The crew slaves were generally well treated and relatively free while with the master and the free crew, but dock workers were supervised in gangs and therefore were more in the category of the plantation slave with regard to treatment. Although available documentation does not mention the extent to which plantation or dock slavery was inhumane, it is reasonable to assume that where gang slavery existed the master-slave relationship was impersonal and treatment was likely to be harsher than in domestic slavery.

There are several reports that African slaves were poorly treated by their Arab masters. While a number of reports stressed whippings, most complaints were of long, hard hours of work and, in other cases, too little food and clothing. The African bondsman responded to his enslavement and poor treatment in a variety of ways, the most dramatic of which were running away or rebelling. It should be noted, however, that there are other, less visible forms of resistance which would not appear in records — work slowdowns, feigned sickness,

26. Bombay, Secret Department, October 12, 1842, pp. 17–26.
27. *Ibid.*

and failure to understand instructions.[28] Although the African response is discussed elsewhere in this study, it is worth emphasizing that the record of African slavery in Asia is one of resistance at many levels and that the struggle for freedom took violent and nonviolent routes.

28. India, External Department, October, 1887, sec. A, pp. 278–93; and *ibid.*, November, 1887, pp. 9–10.

3.

*The Volume
of the Trade*

THE STATISTICAL DATA on the volume of the East African slave trade
is limited primarily to scattered estimates made by British political
agents in East Africa, Arabia, the Persian Gulf, and India, and rough
calculations by European travelers and missionaries. The slave dealers apparently did not keep statistical records; if they did, the information has not become available. It is therefore difficult to gauge the
volume of the African exodus to Asia. The most that can be done is
to seek a rough estimate of the over-all magnitude of the trade during
the nineteenth century, the only period for which there are substantial data. Since even those data are limited, any general estimate must
be regarded as a numbers game, albeit an instructive one.

There are two dimensions of the trade which will be noted at this
point: the direction of the exodus and the number of slaves involved.
With regard to the former, the exodus was primarily to the north and
east, with the heaviest traffic to the Red Sea and Persian Gulf coasts.
Smaller cargoes were transported to India and the islands of the Indian Ocean. With regard to the magnitude of the trade, there are four
significant points at which a count can be taken: the main sources
of slaves, the areas of transit, the markets and ports of embarkation,
and the points of entry abroad.

Sources of Slaves

The southern and western provinces of Ethiopia were major sources
of slaves for the Red Sea traffic. John Krapf estimated that 3,000

slaves were exported annually from the Gurage region during the first half of the nineteenth century. A. Cecchi estimated that in the 1870s Jimma handled 4,000 slaves a year. A decade later an observer estimated that Bonga, another major market in southwestern Ethiopia, handled 8,000 annually. As late as 1907 the Capuchin missionaries calculated that 6,000 to 8,000 slaves were exported annually from Kaffa.[1]

Perhaps the major source of slaves in the heart of the continent was the Bahr el Ghazal, southwest of Ethiopia. C. G. Gordon, governor general of the Sudan, estimated that 80,000 to 100,000 slaves were exported from this area between 1875 and 1879, an average of 20,000 to 25,000 per year for that four-year period.[2] However, there is no way to ascertain how many of those slaves were obtained farther south — for example, from the Great Lakes region. Nor is there any way to determine how many of the 80,000 to 100,000 slaves reached the Red Sea ports, Egypt, or Zanzibar.

Areas of Transit

The second approach to gaining some idea of the extent of the trade is to investigate the areas of transit. The explorer C. T. Beke estimated that in the 1840s 2,000 slaves annually crossed the province of Shoa and no fewer than 7,000 crossed the Blue Nile. Krapf thought that 3,000 to 4,000 slaves annually passed eastward across Shoa to the Gulf of Aden in the first half of the nineteenth century. Capt. W. C. Harris claimed that caravans of up to 3,000 slaves passed through Shoa during most of 1842 and that no fewer than 15,000 to 20,000 slaves passed through the area annually during the 1840s. Guglielmo Massaia heard that about 2,000 slaves were at Ifag in 1851, and Cecchi estimated that 3,000 to 4,000 were annually sold at Rogge, a principal market in Shoa. Massaia also believed that in the 1870s a minimum of 2,000 slaves annually traveled through Shoa

1. Richard Pankhurst, "The Ethiopian Slave Trade in the Nineteenth and Early Twentieth Centuries: A Statistical Inquiry," *Journal of Semitic Studies*, IX, no. 1 (Spring, 1964), 222–23.

2. G. B. Hill, *Colonel Gordon in Central Africa* (London, 1887), p. 369.

in spite of the increased attempts to curtail the trade during the second half of the nineteenth century.[3]

Calculations of the number of slaves secured from the interior and marched across transit areas are even more difficult to make for the southern region because there were fewer explorers and observers than in the northern region, and they traveled less frequently and at a later time. The best figures are from the last half of the nineteenth century, but even those are for scattered years and are not well concentrated as to area. Christopher Rigby, for example, told David Livingstone in the 1850s that 19,000 slaves legally entered Zanzibar from the area around Lake Nyasa. Over a period of thirty days in 1873, British Vice-Consul Frederic Elton saw 4,096 slaves marching north from Tanganyika; he saw more than 1,280 in one week.[4] British Consul Henry O'Neill reported similar figures. But the evidence is insufficient even to suggest an estimate for a single year.

Markets and Ports of Embarkation

The third approach — to investigate the markets and ports of embarkation — is more helpful in formulating a rough estimate of the volume of the trade. The documentation here is greater and more continuous. Furthermore, this approach focuses on the centers to which the major caravan routes led — the final points at which the slaves were gathered before their shipment overseas.

One of the most important markets and ports of embarkation on the Red Sea was Massawa. One observer reported the arrival there of 324 slaves between July 10 and September 10, 1857; 559 between February 6 and July 4, 1858; and 506 between January 8 and September 11, 1859. T. Heuglin estimated that between 1,000 and 1,500 slaves were exported from Massawa in 1861. The missionary A. Haussman estimated that 3,000 were exported in 1862. In 1872 Werner

3. Pankhurst, "Ethiopian Slave Trade," pp. 222–23; and Bombay, Secret Department, May 17, 1843, p. 12.

4. India, Political Department, September, 1878, sec. A, pp. 13–24; Charles E. B. Russell, *General Rigby, Zanzibar and the Slave Trade* (London, 1935), p. 127; and Edward Hutchinson, *The Slave Trade of East Africa* (London, 1874), p. 60.

Munzinger, the governor of Massawa, calculated that in spite of the attempts to curtail the trade about 1,000 slaves per year were being exported. French Consul De Sarzec reported the arrival in Massawa of 500 slaves in 1872 and added that a eunuch of the Egyptian Queen Mother had come to purchase 200 eunuchs and slaves.[5] These unofficial figures range from 1,000 to 3,000 per year, while official estimates are between 600 and 1,000.[6] The latter figures are very likely low, however, because officials were unable to account for all slaves.

The number of slaves who were marched through Shoa to the more southern Red Sea and Gulf of Aden ports — mainly Beilul, Tajura, Roheita, and Zeila — seems to have been substantially higher than the number of slaves who were sent to Massawa. Paul Soleillet reported seeing two caravans arrive in Beilul in 1884, one with 1,200 slaves and the other with 1,500. He believed that such numbers entered Beilul at least every three months. If this estimate is accepted, then between 10,000 and 11,000 slaves arrived at Beilul annually. Writing about ten years later, Oreste Baratieri believed that only about 1,000 were exported from Beilul yearly.[7] It is difficult to reconcile these two reports; Baratieri's figures are smaller than the number of slaves in either of the two caravans Soleillet saw during a short period of 1884. This may well be due to rising and falling demands or successful or unsuccessful collecting parties.

Captain Harris estimated that in the 1840s 3,000 slaves were exported annually from Tajura, while E. F. Berlioux placed the figure at 1,000 per year. Berlioux also esimated that about 4,000 were exported from Zeila in 1870. But in 1884 Soleillet estimated that between 6,000 and 8,000 slaves arrived in Zeila annually.[8] Although Soleillet was concerned with arrivals, Tajura was principally an export market and most of the arrivals would have been sent abroad.

An official report for 1888 provides the following figures for the

5. Pankhurst, "Ethiopian Slave Trade," pp. 224–25.

6. For some official estimates, see E. Blondeel van Cuelebroeck, *Rapport général de Blondeel sur son expédition in Abyssinie* (Brussels, 1839), apps. 17, 19, 28, 33; and Pierre V. A. Ferret and Joseph G. Galinier, *Voyage en Abyssinie* (Paris, 1847–48), I, 329, 331.

7. Pankhurst, "Ethiopian Slave Trade," pp. 225–26.

8. *Ibid.*, p. 226.

Red Sea and Gulf of Aden ports: 1,600 slaves exported from Tajura, 1,000 from Roheita, and 2,000 from Beilul.[9] To repeat, however, official figures are necessarily low; for one thing, they do not account for smuggling, which an unofficial observer can better estimate. In addition, the official report does not include the very active ports of Massawa, Suakin, Berbera, and Zeila.

There are also some revealing figures for the area around Zanzibar. Brig. W. M. Coghlan estimated in 1861 that more than 30,000 slaves were exported annually from the areas under Portugal's and Zanzibar's control. This coincides with other contemporary accounts. Consular reports show that between 1862 and 1867, 97,203 slaves were exported from Kilwa: 76,703 to Zanzibar and 20,500 elsewhere. Therefore, in this five-year period Kilwa legally exported over 15,000 slaves to Zanzibar and over 4,000 elsewhere, for a total annual average of close to 20,000. Consul Churchill estimated that between 3,000 and 4,000 slaves were smuggled annually from the mainland to Zanzibar, which would give Zanzibar an annual intake of between 18,000 and 19,000. Rigby believed that 16,000 were re-exported from Zanzibar each year. This would mean that an estimated 20,000 slaves were exported annually from Zanzibar and Kilwa (16,000 and 4,000, respectively) between 1862 and 1867. In addition, Consul MacLeod estimated in 1857 that 14,000 slaves were exported from Mozambique in three months.[10] Since peak periods varied, the figure of 14,000 was not reached every three months.

Despite the temptation to make an over-all estimate of the volume of the trade, the documentation available at this time is not sufficient to provide the basis for arriving at a meaningful figure. Data are not available for many of the major sources and points of embarkation of slaves. The figures that are available do not provide much continuity and are inconclusive, even for one-year periods. There is no way to determine how many times a slave was counted by official

9. India, Secret Department, August 16, 1889, sec. E, pp. 68–80.

10. Great Britain, Foreign Office, Vol. 84 (*Slave Trade*, Vol. 1019), Russell to Rigby, February 19, 1861, and MacLeod to F.O., October 3, 1857; Hutchinson, *Slave Trade*, p. 38; and India, Secret Department, August 16, 1889, sec. E, pp. 68–70.

and unofficial observers. Finally, there is no basis whatsoever to estimate the number of slaves who were smuggled out of Africa.

An estimate made by the British consul general that 30,000 slaves were exported from Red Sea ports in the 1870s and Richard Pankhurst's calculation that 25,000 were exported during that period from the same general area do not seem unreasonable in light of the evidence presented in this study.[11] Moreover, as was stated earlier, it has been estimated that Zanzibar and Kilwa exported 20,000 slaves annually to non-African areas from 1862 to 1867. Coghlan calculated that over 30,000 were exported during the 1860s from Zanzibar and Mozambique. Acceptance of Coghlan's figures and the figures for Zanzibar and Kilwa would mean that about 10,000 slaves were exported annually from Mozambique during the 1860s; and, in view of the foregoing evidence, that estimate does not seem unreasonable. In fact, Consul MacLeod's report for a three-month period in 1857 presented a much higher figure. Therefore, if one accepts these estimates for the Red Sea area and for the Zanzibar-Mozambique area, the total estimate would be close to 60,000 slaves exported annually from East Africa around 1870.

Asian Points of Entry

With regard to the Asian ports, there are several official calculations of slaves entering Arabia and the Persian Gulf area. Official records for 1820–44 show the following annual estimates of slaves imported into three ports: Bushire, 275; Lingeh, 365; and Bandar Abbas, 320; for a total of 960. An official register kept for a portion of the 1830 season estimated that 1,217 slaves entered Kuwait, Basra, and Mohumorah. Maj. David Wilson, a former British resident in the Persian Gulf, calculated in 1831 that 300 slaves entered Bahrein and vicinity. Lt. A. B. Kemball, another British resident in the Persian Gulf, estimated in 1831 that about 3,488 slaves entered Persia annually; but that figure does not include the very active port of Mus-

11. Richard Gray, *A History of the Southern Sudan, 1839–1889* (Oxford, 1961), p. 182; and Richard Pankhurst, *An Introduction to the Economic History of Ethiopia* (London, 1961), p. 388.

cat, where the sultan maintained stricter control over the trade and restricted the entrance of outside observers.[12]

For the 1840s Major Wilson reported that 1,400 to 1,700 slaves entered Muscat annually, while V. Fontanier, a French traveler and adventurer, estimated a yearly importation of about 4,000 for Muscat and 300 to 400 each for Basra and Bushire. Dr. T. Mackenzie calculated that as many as 4,000 of the slaves brought to Muscat and Sur from Zanzibar were sold annually in the Persian Gulf area. Another observer, Commodore G. B. Brucks, believed that 4,000 to 5,000 Africans were imported into Muscat per year and that 700 to 1,000 of them were Abyssinians. He also estimated that about 1,000 were taken to Sind, Cutch, Kathiawar, and other parts of India each year. Karachi received an estimated 700 to 800 per year. During the 1860s the estimates of slaves imported into Muscat, Basra, Bushire, and Hodeida were about 4,000 each, while an official report of 1871 gives annual figures as high as 12,000 to 15,000 for Jedda.[13]

At least two points should be stressed regarding these Asian estimates. First, the figures are very general, scattered, and probably low, as official counts seem to be. Second, and vitally important, there does not seem to be any way of assuring that a given slave was not counted several times. Of the estimated 12,000 to 15,000 slaves annually imported into Jedda, many were probably reshipped to Bushire, Muscat, and other places. The only available records which confirm this are the very few statements from slaves indicating the various places where they were sold. Because of this insurmountable problem regarding estimates, it is impossible at this stage of research to establish even a rough calculation of the number of Africans actually imported into Asia during the nineteenth century. Adding to this difficulty is the lack of figures on fatalities during the sea voy-

12. Bombay, Miscellaneous Information Connected with the Persan Gulf, n.s., no. 24 (1856), "Paper Relative to the Measures Adopted by the British Government, between the Years 1820 and 1844, for Effecting the Suppression of the Slave Trade in the Persian Gulf," prepared by Lt. A. B. Kemball, pp. 647–49.

13. Bombay, Political Department, Memo from Willoughby (Bombay Castle), April 10, 1840; Great Britain, Foreign Office, Vol. 84 (*Slave Trade*, Vol. 387), Mackenzie to Reid, October 16, 1840, p. 93; *Ibid.* (Vol. 501), Brucks to Aberdeen, October 5, 1842; Bombay, Political Department, April, 1871, sec. A, pp. 40–51.

ages. Furthermore, there is no way to determine how many Africans died during the Asian march from the coast, during the stay in the slave markets, and on subsequent marches to other Asian markets. Finally, there is no way to establish how many slaves arrived in Asia via North Africa. Many of those slaves would very likely have come from West Africa, but there seems to be no way to distinguish between East and West Africans sold in Asia. For the most part, African slaves in Asia were regarded as Siddis, Habshis, or Africans; neither their specific ethnic identity nor their specific place of origin was significant to slave dealers or masters.

4.

Restriction
and Abolition

THE EAST AFRICAN slave trade assumed its greatest international significance and attracted the most attention during the period in which several countries abolished the trade from West Africa. By 1808 Denmark, Britain, and the United States had decreed slave traffic illegal. Although it took several decades for those decrees to have substantial practical effects, at least the legal groundwork, which influenced public opinion, had been laid. By the late 1880s the Atlantic traffic in African slaves was virtually suppressed. Although slave cargoes from East Africa were not uncommon in the Atlantic trade, the greatest demand for slaves from Africa's east coast came from Asia; that demand was enhanced during the nineteenth century as European restrictions in northern and western Africa limited the flow of bondsmen to Asia and America.

Oman, Britain,
and Restrictive Treaties

While most European powers acquiesced in the abolition of the trade, Asian sovereigns, committed both to economic gain and to Islam, which recognized the status of slavery as a natural element in society, saw efforts to curtail the slave trade as threats to their religion, economy, and national sovereignty. The key to abolition in this area was Oman, which controlled much of the commerce in the

51

Indian Ocean. Oman claimed, however tenuous in fact, sovereign rights over the slave-exporting Arab and Swahili towns of East Africa and exercised considerable control over the slave-importing areas of Arabia and the Persian Gulf.

The British undertook to eliminate the Asian demand by negotiating agreements with several sheiks on the west coast of the Persian Gulf (1820, 1838, and 1856), with the shah of Persia (1851), and with the king of Mukalla (1863). The British also negotiated restrictive agreements with some of the Somali kings (1855 and 1856). British India was covered by the Abolition Act of 1811, which prohibited the importation of slaves into that area, and the Indian Government Act of 1843 abolished the legal status of slavery in India. Britain also exerted pressure on the kings of Cutch and Kathiawar, Indian states not then under British rule, to curtail the traffic.

Around 1820, Sir Robert Farquhar, governor of Mauritius, tried to persuade the sultan at Muscat, who was also sultan of Zanzibar, to suppress the slave trade in exchange for special commercial privileges for Muscat vessels. This may have helped pave the way for the Moresby Treaty of 1822, in which the sultan agreed to prohibit "all external traffic in slaves," particularly the sale of slaves to Christians. British cruisers were permitted to seize any Arab slave vessel east or south of a line drawn from Cape Delgado in East Africa, passing two degrees east of Socotra Island, to Diu, in India. This treaty did not seriously affect the main flow of the trade and was therefore not a main concession on the part of the sultan, who saw the agreement as a way of maintaining good relations with England, whose commercial and military influence in the Indian Ocean was increasing perceptibly. By accepting the Moresby Treaty, however, the sultan conceded the negotiability of the trade and in principle recognized British rights in the area. Nevertheless, it was virtually impossible for British cruisers, even when assigned the task, to prevent Arab dhows from sailing into numerous creeks, from dashing into inlets, and from continuing across the patrolled Red Sea or even parts of the Indian Ocean during favorable winds. Furthermore, overland trade continued to supply slaves to the coast. Until the British developed a stronger commitment to the abolition of the slave trade, the overseas demand was met through an illicit traffic. In fact, the commercial treaties negotiated with Oman by the United States (1833), Britain (1839), and France (1844) actually strengthened the sultan's resistance to abolition by expanding commercial relations with powers whose citizens still engaged in the profitable trade.

By 1845, however, the sultan realized that British friendship and sea power had been decisive factors in the establishment and maintenance of his power and influence over parts of Arabia and East Africa and could be useful against possible challenges from the French, whose commercial activities in the Indian Ocean were increasing. Therefore, in spite of the tremendous source of revenue from the slave trade, the sultan acquiesced to British pressure to curtail the export of slaves from his African possessions. The traffic could continue between the mainland and Zanzibar but not overseas — not even to the Arabian territories. While this agreement helped to check the flow of slaves abroad, it could not stop the lucrative business entirely. In fact, by mid-century the French *engagé* system greatly increased the flow of African bondsmen to the Mascarene Islands.[1]

David Livingstone
and Abolition

The abolitionist cause received added momentum in the 1850s from David Livingstone, who in 1851 saw the Arab slave trade firsthand and concluded that the only way to abolish it was through the cooperative efforts of traders and missionaries in the African interior. He believed that settlements of Christian merchants and farmers around a mission station would convince Africans that slaves could be profitably replaced as a trading commodity by produce and other items, that Europeans were eager to purchase those items (cotton, for example), that a combination of agriculture and trade could form the basis for a stable community, and that Christianity could provide the spiritual bond for that community. In sum, Livingstone, not unlike other Europeans who supported similar schemes in West Africa,

1. See pp. 9–10 above.

believed that Europeans could demonstrate to Africans that sedentary, commercially viable Christian settlements in the interior of Africa were wholesome and would eliminate the main evils of the Africans' lives — ignorance, poverty, and fear — all, in his view, closely related to the slave trade. He won many European supporters for this project through his vivid descriptions of the horrors of the slave trade and his exhortations that Christianity was Africa's greatest hope. The remainder of his life was devoted to that cause, and after his death, in 1873, many missionaries and others continued his efforts. The British Anti-Slavery Society, inspired by Livingstone's example, rededicated itself to abolition of the trade and was largely responsible for the dispatch of Sir Bartle Frere, former governor of Bombay, as special envoy to Zanzibar and Muscat to investigate the trade and make recommendations to the British government. In 1873, a few weeks after Livingstone's death in Africa, Frere negotiated the treaty which marked the legal end of the Arab slave trade.

The Moresby Treaty of 1822 had obliged the sultan to prohibit the slave trade in areas outside his African and Asian territories, and the agreement of 1845 had committed him to limit the trade to the coastal traffic between Zanzibar and his other African possessions. But the Treaty of 1873 bound him to curtail the trade by sea entirely and obliged him to close the slave markets in his dominions. The enforcement of those treaties, however, was essentially the responsibility of the British navy, which was never fully committed to the task.

Manumission
and Settlements

Another approach to abolishing the trade was the manumission of slaves in various parts of Asia by local chiefs and British political officers.[2] A new dimension was added in 1873, when Frere suggested that, with the exception of freed girls in the Asylum of the Roman Catholic Sisters of Mercy in Aden and former slaves living with a few "respectable and responsible" private families in the same city, lib-

2. See Chapter 5.

erated Africans should be returned to East Africa. Very likely he was favorably impressed by the West African examples of Sierra Leone and Liberia. Frere noted that the objectives of liberating slaves should be: to settle them in proximity to their original home, or at least in a similar climate; to stimulate their self-reliance, thereby laying the foundation for "free, self-sustaining communities"; and to "civilize" them through education. All of this, Frere argued, could be achieved without inordinate expense to the British treasury.[3]

The places to which Frere recommended that liberated Africans be sent were the Universities Mission and the French Roman Catholic mission at Zanzibar and Bagamoyo, several Church Missionary Society (CMS) missions, and the proposed Universities Mission at Dar es Salaam. In 1874 Rev. William S. Price, who had founded the African Asylum at Nasik (discussed in the next chapter), established Freretown on the East African coast near Mombasa, under the auspices of the Church Missionary Society of London. He became the first superintendent and continued the work he had started at Nasik. Freretown was to be a center for training teachers and missionaries for CMS missions in various parts of East Africa. Industrial education also was to be provided. Price was assisted by Mathew Wellington, a liberated African who had been trained by Price at Nasik. Since Wellington and other early settlers in Freretown and in subsequent communities for liberated Africans on the coast had returned from the Bombay area, they became known as "Bombay Africans." Over 150 of them emigrated from Bombay in 1875, following the closing of the Asylum at Nasik.[4]

Zanzibar was another area in which the British hoped to resettle Africans. A. H. Hardinge, British agent and consul general at Zanzibar, reported to Lord Salisbury that the Zanzibar government wanted to procure plantation labor and was prepared in general to find employment for liberated Africans. Hardinge suggested that those liberated be handled in lots of fifty. It was proposed that some of them

3. India, Secret Department, June, 1873, pp. 236, 311.

4. *Proceedings of the Church Missionary Society* (1867–68), pp. 49–50. See also Professor A. J. Temu's paper, "The Role of the Bombay Africans (Liberated Africans) on the Mombasa Coast, 1874–1904," which was read at the Kenya Historical Conference in 1969.

receive holdings on government estates in Zanzibar and Pemba. In return they would be required to give eight hours' free labor per week on the estates. The remaining time could be used to cultivate their own holdings for their personal benefit. Other freedmen could work for the government at the regular wage of free laborers. If this choice were made, the liberated Africans would receive a suit of clothes at the beginning of each clove season, regular rations during picking season, and a gratuity equal to a week's pay at the end of Ramadan, the Muslim fast. Other jobs were available with private European merchants; those occupations provided no lodging, but the workers received a regular daily wage according to the contract. The sultan agreed with these procedures. In addition, neighboring Mombasa reportedly wanted 100 carriers and laborers for the railroad company and the Public Works and Shipping Department. While there were possibilities of work on plantations, the government did not supervise them and therefore could not make any labor arrangements.[5]

In order to check the considerable flow of Somali slaves being exported annually from the area around Lamu, Frere proposed the establishment of a free African settlement somewhere on the Somali coast. He recommended similar communities for Kilwa and the area south of the Ruvuma River, near the Portuguese colony of Mozambique. These settlements were to be patterned after Freretown and were expected to provide refuge for runaway slaves as well as a stable Christian community for Africans in general.[6]

Another location endorsed by Frere was Mauritius, where the governor, Sir Arthur Gorden, estimated that 200 to 400 adults could be settled each year. This was simply the continuation of a practice that had already been adopted. Since the 1820s African slaves and quasi-free laborers in Mauritius had worked as calkers, divers, boatmen, and messengers; some also worked in civil and military stores. African children received some education at Reduit and Mon Plaisir. In July, 1869, a French mail agent in Mauritius, Henri Richard, requested that Bombay send 15 manumitted slaves to work on the island. After receiving them, he requested an additional 30. This led to

5. India, External Department, August, 1897, sec. A, pp. 17–24.
6. India, Secret Department, June, 1873, p. 311.

an agreement between the British governments in Mauritius and India that 200 to 300 ex-slaves be shipped to the island as free labor. The government undertook no costs, so Richard arranged for shipping and other expenses. The Africans were informed of the arrangements and were told that in case of mistreatment they could appeal to the Mauritius government. No African was to be sent forcibly. A year later the colonial secretary of Mauritius reported that the original 15 Africans had been contracted for five years on the docks at the government's rate of wages and allowances.[7]

In January, 1875, Capt. W. F. Prideaux, British consul general at Zanzibar, sent the government of India a report in which he noted that training and education were provided for African children, who constituted a majority of the slaves captured by British cruisers and landed at Mahé (Seychelles). An archdeacon was in charge of the CMS mission receiving the youths. But, according to Prideaux, labor was needed to make the island prosperous.

> It is only on the importation of Africans that they [clove and tropical fruit plantations] can rely for the development of the resources of the island. . . . [The Africans] take a pride in assuming European customs.[8]

Prideaux stressed his belief in the superiority of European customs and the desirability of "civilizing" Africans:

> It is impossible not to feel that they [liberated Africans] have risen several degrees higher in the scale of civilization than those who have been left within the range of Eastern influence.[9]

This argument was in support of labor contracts for five years in Mauritius.

Documentation is too sparse at this point to estimate the number of liberated Africans who settled in Mauritius or the much larger number who were imported there as slaves. But it is not unlikely that

7. Bombay, Political Department, March, 1870, sec. A, pp. 81–87; and *Irish University Press Series of British Parliamentary Paper* (Shannon, 1969), *Slave Trade*, LXXVI, 516–18.

8. India, Political Department, May, 1875, sec. A, pp. 406–10.

9. *Ibid.*

tens of thousands voluntarily and involuntarily adopted the island as home.

Several Englishmen recommended other sites for liberated African slaves: Johanna Island and South Africa, where the demand was great for domestics and laborers.[10] Even Liberia, in spite of its great distance, was suggested. But by the late nineteenth century the prevailing sentiment supported Frere's aim to establish communities as near as possible to places from which African slaves had originally been taken. A good deal of additional research needs to be conducted to determine the approximate number of liberated Africans who were returned to Africa, but present evidence suggests that the number was small.

The Brussels Conference
of 1889

The evidence is clear that the gradual suppression of the slave trade in both East and West Africa resulted primarily from the efforts of Britishers, who increasingly received the support of their government. Some of the abolitionists undoubtedly were sincere and believed their cause was just; others very likely saw in the movement an opportunity for material gain and the enhancement of their prestige. The slave trade had developed in response to the expanding economic designs of European countries in the fifteenth and sixteenth centuries, with Britain the major participant when the slave trade was at its peak. It is somewhat ironic that several hundred years later the same European economy, much more highly developed and worldwide, provided the stimulus through industrialism and capitalism that led to the abolition of the trade, and that Britain, the commercial pacesetter in the nineteenth century, responded most vigorously to those times.

By the 1890s, however, several European countries had developed a keen interest in the economic and political future of Africa. Parti-

10. This was the period (the second half of the nineteenth century) in which Indian laborers were being taken to Natal to build railroads and work on plantations.

tion, colonialism, and imperialism were the trends of the times, and because commerce was a major objective, stability and law and order were required; consequently, the slave trade had to be abolished. These were also times when Europeans were committed to "the white man's burden," and saw Christianity as a way of "civilizing" Africans. The dehumanizing slave trade had to be stopped and Christian brotherhood had to be taught. It is thus clear that major forces at work both inside and outside of Africa opposed the slave trade.

Thus European efforts to abolish the slave trade paved the way for the Brussels Conference of 1889. While the Berlin Conference of 1884–85 had dealt with the issue of slavery and the slave trade in only a peripheral way, the Brussels Conference aimed to put "an end to the crimes and devastation engendered by the traffic in African slaves." The result was the ratification of a General Act in which the representative countries agreed to suppress the trade by controlling the areas in which it originated, by intercepting and freeing slave caravans, and by forbidding the importation of slaves into areas controlled by the signatories. The General Act also sought to suppress the prevalent use of foreign flags on vessels engaged in the trade by declaring that all users of foreign colors must prove that they had never been condemned for slave trading. (Ships sailing under foreign flags enjoyed the exemptions of extraterritoriality and could not be prosecuted by local authorities.) In order to prevent the transportation of slaves under the guise of African crewmen, the act provided that "a list of the crew shall be issued to the captain of the vessel at the port of departure by the authorities of the power whose colors it carries."

> No Negro can be engaged as a seaman on a vessel without having been beforehand questioned by the authority of the Power whose color it carries, or, in default thereof, by the territorial authority, with a view to ascertain the fact of his having contracted a free engagement.[11]

Similarly, if a captain wanted to carry black passengers, he was required to declare them to the power whose flag he carried. The pas-

11. India, External Department, June, 1891, sec. A, Art. XXXV.

sengers involved were then asked if they had embarked of their own free will, and, if this was the case, the vessel's manifest would indicate it. No black children were to be admitted as passengers unless accompanied by adults.[12] These were all crucial provisions if the slave trade were to be effectively suppressed.

The Effectiveness
of the General Act of 1890

Like all previous agreements on this subject, the General Act lacked any effective enforcement procedures and relied heavily on the integrity of the signatories, as well as that of other countries. The greatest problem came from the French, who had not accepted the agreement. The British officials in the Persian Gulf frequently reported that Frenchmen were encouraging and participating in the illicit traffic. Slave dhows flying French flags were observed in Ottoman, Persian, and Zanzibar waters; all of them claimed the privileges of extraterritoriality enjoyed by French-owned vessels. This immunity from practical control by local authorities very seriously challenged all attempts to suppress the slave trade. Also, in several cases Suri Arabs obtained French flags and certifying papers from French consuls at African and Asian ports, which allowed them to transport slaves into the sultan's Asian territory.[13] By the mid-1890s British apprehension over this French policy had increased. In a secret communication of 1895, the British resident in the Persian Gulf reported considerable importation of slaves into Oman by Suri dhows flying French flags. Indian merchants also reported that Suri dhows under French colors were landing slaves at Sur and along the Batinah coast. Those dhows allegedly were registered by French agents at Obok (French Somaliland) and Madagascar. A French consul, M. P. Ottavi, was reported as a source of French flags for Suri dhows. One captured dhow with thirty-three slaves had French papers authorizing it to trade between Madagascar, the adjacent islands, and the

12. *Ibid.*
13. India, Secret Department, July, 1892, sec. E, pp. 24-45.

African coast. Another captured vessel had French papers authorizing trade in the Persian Gulf; the buyers were reportedly Bedouins, who marched the slaves overland to the Batinah coast.[14]

In 1890 the British commander, C. J. Baker, reported an increase in slave importation into Sur, and said the majority of the slaves spoke Swahili and were believed to have come from areas around Mozambique and Madagascar. He stated that some 300 dhows flying French colors were engaged in the trade. Baker reported that the sultan of Oman explained that his subjects went to Africa and Aden and obtained French flags on the ground that they resided in French territories. In 1899 some 58 vessels owned by subjects of the sultan were still listed as flying French flags. On hearing that 500 slaves had been collected at Tajura for shipment to Arabia, E. H. Egerton, British minister to Paris, inquired about the French position on the subject. The French replied that their colonial authorities were seriously repressing the slave trade throughout the French protectorate (Somaliland).[15] But as late as 1898 the India Office in London reported that French authorities would not admit that slave dhows flew French flags. However, reports continued to identify the misuse of French colors. A Captain Cook, who said he once commanded cruisers for the Turkish Tobacco Company, reported that he had caught several slave dhows, most of them flying French flags.[16]

After having signed the Treaty of 1873, Barghash, the Zanzibar sultan, unswervingly supported the British efforts to suppress the traffic. At the turn of the century he made this request:

I have the honor to address you regarding the matter of the French flags which are handed about among my subjects, inhabitants of Sur, and elsewhere. . . . I am much vexed with regard to it, as it is detrimental both to my independence and to my prestige. . . . There have been quarrels among sections of my subjects over this matter. . . . If your great Government can see the way to discuss the question with the great French Government on my behalf, with a view to effecting the removal of the flags now in use and the dis-

14. *Ibid.*, March, 1893, pp. 2–27, 175–79; *ibid.*, February, 1895, pp. 438–53; and *ibid.*, February, 1897, pp. 28–68.

15. *Ibid.*, March, 1890, pp. 22–27; *ibid.*, July, 1897, pp. 187–222; and *ibid.*, March, 1899, pp. 692–721.

16. *Ibid.*, August, 1899, pp. 101–5.

continuance of the practice, I shall be extremely grateful and obliged.[17]

By this time, however, the slave traffic had diminished greatly and within a few years was no longer a major international issue.[18]

Indians
in the Slave Trade

Another group of persistent participants in the East African slave trade was the Indians. Though they were of less consequence than the Arabs and the French, they were, nonetheless, significant partners in the trade. In 1853 Major Hammerton, British consul and government agent at Muscat, reported to the British government in Bombay that a lively slave trade was being conducted between Zanzibar and the Indian states of Cutch and Kathiawar, the regions from which most Indian participants in the trade seem to have come. The evidence is limited, but it is clear that Ebjee Sewjee, a Cutchee who was a brother of Iairain Sewjee, the customs master of Zanzibar, sought to establish a slave-trading business in the southern area of East Africa, and in 1853 he went to Cutch to establish connections there for the trade. Ebjee Sewjee's efforts, as well as those of two other Cutchees who attempted a similar venture, failed. There were, however, several Cutchees in Zanzibar who became wealthy from the slave trade. Major Hammerton suggested that they would not engage in the trade if their property and persons were made liable in Cutch.[19]

In May, 1860, Lt. Col. Christopher Rigby, British consul and agent at Zanzibar, reported that a banian, Kanru Munjee, a long-time resident of Zanzibar, had extensive relations with Arabs and others involved in the slave trade. He owned a plantation on the island and had sixty-nine slaves. He was arrested, fined, and assessed money for each slave's support as well as for land for each child.[20]

17. *Ibid.*, September, 1900, p. 18.
18. *Ibid.*, September, 1903, pp. 336, 383.
19. Bombay, Political Department, December 2, 1853, pp. 98–100.
20. *Ibid.*, May, 1860, sec. A, pp. 286–91.

Another Indian, Kesu Gokaldass, was found guilty of dealing in slaves and was fined and banished from Zanzibar by the consular court. The consul general at Zanzibar requested that the Gokaldass case be published in the native Gujarati newspapers, which were also read by Cutchees in Zanzibar. The consul thought that this publicity might convince Zanzibar Cutchees that the Cutch government and the British government in India would punish future offenders.[21] Indeed, British pressure on the rao (king) of Cutch moved him to issue a proclamation warning his subjects against dealing in slaves in Zanzibar or any other place. The rao declared that anyone who violated the proclamation would be liable to punishment on return to Cutch. The British cordially approved the proclamation and had it distributed in Arabic and Gujarati to the various Cutchee communities.[22]

For several years the Cutchee community in Zanzibar had been undergoing a change of loyalty. They had initially preferred British protection because it gave them international status and commercial advantages with the British merchants who dominated Zanzibar's trade. But as the British increasingly restricted the slave trade, the Cutchees began to attach themselves to the sultan, who benefited from and therefore sought to preserve the slave trade. Thus, from the late 1860s most Cutchees regarded themselves as being subject to the sultan rather than to the British. The Zanzibar sultan, Syeed Majid, regarded the rao's proclamation as a means of dividing his subjects by making them liable to punishment by the rao. To make matters worse for the sultan, the rao in 1872 delegated jurisdiction to the British in cases where Cutchees were offenders in Zanzibar.[23] A year later the problem was resolved when the sultan signed the Treaty of 1873.

A Cutchee, Bohra Muhammadbhai Alibhai, owned a vessel which carried both Cutch and French flags. Its slaving activities were limited mainly to the French-controlled waters around Madagascar. Another Indian shipowner, Tulshi Narsi, of Jodia in the Navanagar province of Kathiawar, settled in Madagascar, where he engaged in the trade. Narsi was only one of several Hindu and Muslim Indians

21. India, Political Department, July, 1874, pp. 264–73.
22. Bombay, Political Department, January, 1870, sec. A, pp. 4–45.
23. *Ibid.*; and India, Political Department, September, 1873, sec. A, pp. 248–51.

of Navanagar to establish residence in French-African colonies in order to participate freely in the business of slaving.[24]

Although a good deal of additional research is needed to determine the extent of Indian involvement in the slave trade, by the turn of the century Indian participation could not have been significant. By then the trade was declining, and even the French were becoming more vigilant in curtailing the traffic.

When the government in India received word in March, 1903, that a Portuguese ship had captured twelve Suri dhows and rescued 700 slaves, Maj. P. Z. Cox wrote the following message to the British political resident in the Persian Gulf:

> I have consistently maintained that there has been little or no practical diminution in the annual consignments of human beings shipped from East Africa to Sur and the vicinity; in which direction the Arabian and Persian Gulf markets look for their regular supply of slaves.[25]

The following year Cox, then the officiating political resident in the Persian Gulf, wrote as follows to the Indian government:

> The attitude of the Navy in regard to slavery in these waters is not a very genuine one in my experience of the last few years. . . . The whole time I was at Maskat not a single piece of genuine and serious slave-cruising was done, much less was any slave dhow captured; and the way they satisfy their consciences, or fulfill their orders in this direction, is often most perfunctory.[26]

These two reports may exaggerate the extent of the traffic at that time, but scattered references in official documents to small numbers of Africans being captured on the seas or sold in various parts of Asia support the fact that the trade continued well into the twentieth century; indeed, there are reports that it continues on a small scale even today.

24. India, Secret Department, March, 1899, sec. E, pp. 692–721.
25. *Ibid.*, September, 1903, p. 249.
26. *Ibid.*, February, 1905, p. 8.

5.

Provinces of Freedom

In SPITE of the various treaties Britain negotiated for the abolition of slavery in the nineteenth century and in spite of British efforts to secure manumission in both Asia and parts of East Africa, slavery and the trade continued. There were several reasons for this: The holding of slaves was not prohibited by the Treaty of 1873; the demand continued to exist; slave dealers were persistent; and enforcement by the navy was not effective, although a few thousand slaves were caught and freed.

One of the approaches Britain used to suppress the slave trade was to free slaves and settle them in separate Asian communities. This was done by Asian rulers and British consuls. An Arab ruler would occasionally free a slave who had demonstrated unusual heroism in battle or who had saved the life of a relative or friend or one who had been treated with unusual cruelty by a master. Freedom in the latter instance often resulted from pressure by British consuls and political agents. The procedure which developed during the nineteenth century was for the slave to make a statement to the British consul that he was badly treated by his master or that he had been brought into the country illegally.[1] An investigation by the consul would follow the slave's testimony, or the case would be presented to the local king for an investigation. In either case the local sovereign was informed and his judgment sought. When the decision was favorable to the slave, a manumission certificate was issued by British of-

---

1. See Appendix 1.

ficials. This certificate usually showed the freedman's name and the place, date, and authority of his liberation. The freedman was required to have this document in his possession at all times, and it was to be honored by all British legations and all sovereigns whose area was covered by an abolition agreement with Britain.[2]

Life as an African freedman in Asia presented many problems, including the need for employment, food and housing, education, and general security. No serious attention was given to these matters until abolition agreements had been negotiated. Consequently, several consular offices found themselves responsible for the welfare of a number of liberated Africans. Although the British allowed the use of some consular funds for this situation, it became obvious that a constructive plan had to be devised for the general welfare of the freedmen. Supported by small grants from the British treasury and the East India Company, consuls provided some initial assistance to freedmen in the way of food and clothing and helped to find them employment or to place them with "respectable" families. Most of the African women were placed in domestic situations, while the men acquired jobs as sailors, dock workers, porters, or general laborers. African children were usually sent to mission orphanages until they were old enough to care for themselves. In general, these were the procedures followed to varying degrees in Bahrein, Bandar Abbas, Mauritius, Baghdad, Constantinople, Muscat, Basra, Aden, Nasik and Bombay. This chapter will focus on manumission and related developments in Aden, Bombay, and Nasik.

Aden

Because of its harbor, its proximity to the East African coast, and its favorable location with regard to the monsoon winds, Aden was selected by England as one of three depots for Africans liberated from dhows captured on the Red Sea or the Indian Ocean. The other two depots were Bombay and the Seychelles. The captain of a cruiser could decide which depot was the closest and best situated to receive

2. India, Secret Department, April, 1913, sec. E, p. 161; *ibid.*, November, 1908, p. 287; and Bombay, Political Department, August, 1871, sec. A, pp. 28–41.

his shipment of freedmen. Aden also received some Africans who were liberated in other parts of Arabia. The settlement area of Aden was about fifteen square miles, but more than half of it was uninhabitable. It was located on an island in the inner harbor, about two miles from the town. Food and water had to be conveyed there by boat. Although the settlement was isolated, there was always fear that the Africans would spread some contagious disease they had contracted on the cramped dhows. An apothecary or hospital assistant was appointed for medical care, and a regular medical officer made weekly visits to the settlement.[3]

The British resident was responsible for finding employment for the freedmen. Most received jobs as domestics with "respectable natives of India resident in Aden." Some were employed with the Harbor Department, others secured jobs with the Peninsula and Oriental Shipping Company, and several found work as sailors on private dhows. The young freedmen were usually placed in mission schools operated by the Roman Catholic Sisters of Mercy or the Church of Scotland mission, both in Aden. Otherwise there were no schools available to them.[4]

From 1865 to 1870, the number of African freedmen who landed in Aden was as follows: 1865, 249; 1866, 149; 1867, 231; 1868, 524; 1869 to June 30, 1870, 1044; a total of 2,197 for the five-year period.[5] Many Africans entered Aden in 1868, following the British expedition to Ethiopia to secure the release of two detained British envoys, but no record of those refugees was kept. It seems, however, that most of them settled elsewhere in Aden, although it is not unlikely that some of them sought the security of the freedmen's settlement. Other Africans liberated elsewhere in Arabia also gravitated to the community.

As the number of freedmen increased, the problems of health and sanitation, the difficulty in securing food and water, the overcrowded conditions, the need for police supervision, and the scarcity of employment led the resident in 1869 to recommend against locating Afri-

3. Bombay, Political Department, January, 1870, sec. A, pp. 183–89.
4. *Ibid.*
5. *Ibid.*; and India, External Department, September, 1887, sec. A, pp. 135–35a.

cans in Aden. He proposed sending all liberated Africans to Bombay. While the government of India recognized the problem, it maintained that Aden was a convenient depot because of its proximity to the principal area of the slave trade. However, Aden was allowed to send some liberated Africans to Bombay; about 700 were waiting to be shipped there in 1869.[6] After about 1870, Aden served only occasionally as a depot for liberated African slaves being returned to Africa.[7]

Bombay

At least as early as the eighteenth century, the British were involved in the African slave trade to India, primarily to Bombay and neighboring areas. There is evidence that African slaves were used even then in the British navy; but when British cruiser commanders reported that it was impossible to make "Madagascar slaves" useful on board ship, the Council of the United Company of Merchants of England agreed that the slaves could be used as laborers in the marine yard. Africans were also purchased from slaving vessels and trained as calkers for the East India Company, which advertised contract slaves for anyone desirous of such labor. How many contract slaves were involved is difficult to ascertain, but in 1763 some 500 were contracted by a company agent. There were several requests for Madagascar slaves, and these requests were probably met because there are several references in company records showing that provisions were supplied to the "Madagascar slaves."[8]

The great difficulty in studying the history of African slaves in

6. Bombay, Political Department, January, 1870, sec. A, pp. 183–89, Commodore Sir L. Heath to Secretary of Admiralty, March 24, 1869, Encl. nos. 3, 4, p. 65.

7. Because the United States did not have diplomatic relations with Southern Yemen in 1967–68, I was unable to visit Aden and secure information on present-day African settlements there.

8. Bombay, *Public Department Diary*, no. 29 (July, 1756), no. 48 (1767), no. 39 (October 19, 1762), no. 40 (February 21 and March 1, 1763), no. 33 (September 18, 1759). Madagascar was within the area reserved by royal charter to ships of the East India Company. Larger cargoes of Madagascar slaves were shipped to the Americas, especially during the eighteenth century. See Virginia B. Platt, "The East India Company and the Madagascar Slave Trade," *William and Mary Quarterly*, Vol. XXVI (October, 1969).

India is that the records which refer to slaves rarely indicate their origin. Since the British and Indians used both Africans and Indians as bondsmen and since the records show that African and Indian slaves were sometimes referred to collectively as "slaves," the researcher is extremely limited in determining the extent of African slavery. It is clear, however, that the African slave trade contributed to the increasing number of Africans in the Bombay area. In 1759 an official British abstract listing people who could be used to defend Bombay mentioned 754 Siddis from the port city of Surat and 108 African slaves.[9]

By the 1770s "black people" in Bombay had become a particular concern of the English. Over the years, freed and escaped Africans and persons of mixed Arab and African ancestry began to settle in certain sections of Bombay. The British established a committee to investigate the situation because of the "great want of ground within the town for Europeans to build, and the Church Street being a very proper place for that purpose." It was thus resolved "that the present proprietors [blacks] be positively prohibited [from] repairing [their homes] in future, which we hope will be a means of inducing them to sell to Europeans on reasonable terms."[10] This resolution raises questions about the number of Africans in the town, the reasons for migration and concentration in the Church Street area, the number of Europeans involved and the extent of their concern, and how the problem was resolved. An examination of the available records for the next decade failed to provide any answers to these questions.

Documentation for the entry of Africans into India, especially Bombay, improved during the nineteenth century. There was an increase in the number of British East India Company agents, who concerned themselves with the need to suppress the overseas slave trade in order to develop a more effective trade in legitimate goods. As was already pointed out, Mocha and Muscat were among the significant distributing centers for slaves destined for India via the sea. In 1814 Synd Hussin Bin Uhmud Hubushee reported that Uhmud Bin Salim

9. Bombay, *Public Department Diary*, no. 33 (August 7, 1759).

10. *Ibid.*, no. 60 (February 25, 1772). Where the term *black* is used to describe persons in India, care has been taken to assure that they are of African ancestry and not members of any other group such as the Dravidians, whose origins are controversial.

Noemin commanded a dhow to the Malabar Coast and sold four Ethiopians. Eighteen Africans — ten women and eight men — were purchased in Mocha and shipped to Bombay in July, 1833. Two Mughul merchants marched them to Lucknow via Jaipur and Agra and later sold them to the king of Oudh. The vice-consul at Basra, who earlier had served in India, reported that in 1835 he saw a rich Mughul accompanied by about ten Abyssinians; the Mughul allegedly had two eunuchs in Bombay. The vice-consul stated that African males landed at Bombay in women's clothes and passed by the customs officer posing as wives of Arab slave dealers. He concluded that Abyssinian servants in Bombay were very common. In 1836 a native agent of Mocha reported that Arabs smuggled African female slaves into Bombay under the pretence of marriage and sold them to Mughuls. He also reported that the trade from the Persian Gulf to India was vigorous.[11]

I. P. Willoughby, political agent in Kathiawar in 1836, observed that there was no allusion to slavery in his agency's records, suggesting that the subject had not been of importance to his predecessors. However, he saw several African boys in attendance on kings in Kathiawar and, on examination of customs records, confirmed the importation of slaves. This trade was considerable from Muscat and the Persian Gulf, both by sea and by land, to Karachi, Cutch, and Kathiawar. Prior to 1838, for example, it was estimated that not more than 150 African slaves were imported annually into Karachi; but by 1840 the number rose to 1,500. Some of the slave dealers were Arabs, others were Turks, and the rao of Cutch was allegedly involved in the trade. Prices varied, but the highest fees were paid for males between ten and twenty years of age and for females.[12]

By 1840 there were an estimated 996 Africans identified among the 5,338 slaves in Kathiawar.[13] That British officials were concerned about reports of a vigorous African slave trade in India is confirmed

11. *Irish University Press Series of British Parliamentary Papers* (Shannon, 1969), *Slave Trade*, LXXIV, 802; *ibid.*, LXXXVIII, 208; Bombay, Political Department, July 18, 1833, pp. 40–42; *ibid.*, September 19, 1836, p. 30; and *ibid.*, February 13, 1839, p. 30.

12. Bombay, Political Department, September 19, 1836, p. 11; and *Irish University Press, Slave Trade*, LXXXVIII, 212.

13. *Irish University Press, Slave Trade*, LXXXVIII, 202.

by the following proclamation, published in 1839 in English, Persian, Arabic, Gujarati, and Marathi:

> The Governor in Council of Bombay, having reason to believe that the traffic in slaves is carried on to a considerable extent, by persons in Arab boats and vessels from the ports in the Red Sea and Persian Gulf, and other ports, importing slaves of both sexes and of various ages, into the Port of Bombay and the ports and places subordinate to the Presidency of Bombay . . . hereby notifies and proclaims that all persons found guilty of such practices, or in any other manner offending against the laws for the abolition of the slave trade, shall be apprehended and prosecuted. . . . A reward is held out by act of Parliament of . . . £100 sterling for each slave to any person who shall inform and sue and prosecute for the slave.[14]

Along with Aden and the Seychelles, Bombay served as a depot for freed Africans. In fact, many of those manumitted in Aden were subsequently sent to Bombay because it was a larger station and provided greater opportunities for employment. In 1835 over 200 slaves were seized in three Arab vessels at the port of Porbandar in Kathiawar and were subsequently sent to Bombay, where the commissioner of police was instructed to place them in employment, in some charitable institution, or with families. At first only Christian families were sought, but after Muslim Africans refused to live with any but Muslim families, the government honored that choice. Although there was no written agreement, the government stressed the point that the Africans were free and could leave if they wished to do so. The government paid an annual subsidy for each child but nothing for adults.[15]

During the 1830s and 1840s the commissioner of police accepted letters of request for liberated African children from private families who agreed to feed, clothe, and protect them and to pay wages for their services. The government regarded itself as being *in loco parentis* and required each child to appear before a police officer twice a year until his eighteenth birthday. This requirement was a means of keeping check on the location and status of the freed youth. A Mr.

14. Bombay, Political Department, February 13, 1839, p. 30.
15. *Ibid.*, September 19, 1836, pp. 10, 11.

Townsend, who was a secretary to the government, was permitted to take twenty-four of the freed children. He agreed to provide them a home and to send them to school. Since some of them were Muslims, he agreed not to mention religion, but it was hoped that through their associations they would become Christians. In another case, a Capt. J. Henderson was allowed to take four freed African boys as laborers for his estate at the Cape of Good Hope.[16]

In 1836 the advocate general advised the government that freed males could be enlisted in the Indian navy. This practice was increasingly accepted, and within twenty years the secretary to the government of Bombay observed that the majority of "our seamen" on naval vessels were Africans. Many of them were fugitives who had escaped from Arabian and Persian Gulf ports and were liberated by naval officers.[17]

In 1864 the census of Bombay showed 2,074 "Negro-Africans"; others were probably included under the general categories of "Muslim" and "Christian." It is likely that many were not counted in the census, which did not even account for all native Indians. Those of mixed descent were probably not listed as Africans. Of the 2,074, 1,441 gave Africa as their birthplace; 1,076 of them were employed as maritime men or boatmen, 336 as laborers, and the others in a variety of menial jobs.[18]

By the 1870s the procedure for handling the freedmen was as follows. The children were sent to one of the mission schools — the African Asylum (CMS) in Nasik, under Rev. William S. Price; the Roman Catholic orphanage of Bandra; the American mission in Siroor (Poona), under Rev. R. Winsor; or the mission high school in Ahmadnagar, under Rev. James Smith. In these cases the government agreed to contribute a monthly allowance for the children's upkeep. Some of the adult freedmen were employed on the government farm at Khandesh. Others secured jobs in railroad workshops or with private families as domestics. In all cases the Africans were told they were free and could leave whenever they chose. For the most

16. *Ibid.*, p. 11.

17. *Ibid.*, p. 10; and *ibid.*, November 9, 1855, pp. 8–11.

18. Bombay, *Gazetteer of the Bombay Presidency* (Bombay, 1882), XIII, pts. 1, 2, pp. 46–47, 87–97.

part this seems to have been only a noble gesture, since the Africans did not speak the local languages and employment opportunities were few.[19]

By the late 1880s the Bombay police commissioner reported that the number of Africans in the city was considerable, though he did not give any figures, and that they formed an "excitable and turbulent" element in the population. He therefore advised against accepting freedmen; he was of the opinion that they would be "a source of danger." Consequently, the government of India investigated the possibility of diverting the recently manumitted Africans to the Straits Settlements in Fiji and Sarawak and to the North Borneo Company, where labor was needed.[20]

The Fiji Islands government requested additional information before it could make a decision. It wanted to know the mental and physical condition of the freedmen, whether they were orderly and amenable to discipline, and whether they were fit for service as agricultural laborers. The Bombay police commissioner replied that the freedmen were "mostly inferior mentally but not physically" and that they were well behaved and amenable to discipline but not fit for service as agricultural laborers. The political resident in the Persian Gulf described them as "mostly a good type physically and mentally"; he added that many were "of the higher type, as the Abyssinians." The political agent in Muscat noted that the freedmen were "mentally low class, good physique, inclined to good order and fairly amenable to discipline." He also described them as fit for agricultural labor but "somewhat lazy."[21] It is understandable that Fiji and the other governments refused to accept any of the liberated Africans.

Most of the liberated Africans in Bombay were attached to Indian or European families or were placed in schools, missionary stations, government farms, or on the docks. Since the basic objective in each case was to relate Africans to the interests of Europeans or Western-

19. India, External Department, November, 1887, sec. A, p. 182; *idem*, Political Department, June, 1873, sec. A, pp. 360–63; and *idem*, Secret Department, October, 1888, sec. E, pp. 185–88.

20. India, Secret Department, February, 1890, sec. E, pp. 160–62.

21. *Ibid.*, June, 1889, sec E, pp. 76–85; and *idem*, External Department, June, 1890, p. 124.

oriented Indians, and because the Africans were few in number and widely dispersed throughout the city, no sizable community of Africans seems to have emerged in Bombay proper. Moreover, from the 1870s the number of Africans being freed and settling in Bombay declined perceptibly, partly because of the more effective restriction of the slave trade and partly because settlements for liberated Africans were being founded on the East African coast.

Nasik

In 1854 at Nasik, about a hundred miles from Bombay, Rev. William S. Price of the CMS founded the African Asylum, a school and orphanage for Africans. The Asylum was a department of the Indo-British Institution, which was connected with the Trinity Chapel. Ten African boys entered the first year, and two years later, twenty-four entered, when several slaves imported into Karachi were liberated and sent to the Bombay depot. The Bombay government contributed a subsidy which had been levied as fines on the importers. The Bombay commissioner of police reported in 1857 that the Africans received a "suitable education to enable them to earn a livelihood and also receive such moral and religious instruction as will tend to make them good members of the community." The government, recognizing the advantage of such a place for freed African children, awarded a second grant from the public revenue.[22]

The program of instruction included the history of England, the geography of Europe, grammar, arithmetic, and Bible studies. Price hoped that some of his graduates would later enroll in the University of Bombay. The director of public instruction for the government reported that the boys repeated the church catechism "pretty well" but in general were "rather slow, docile boys." He also observed that the boys were "more sympathetic than the clever, precociously reserved Hindu boys that I am used to see [sic] in our elementary vernacular schools."[23]

22. Bombay, Home Department, April 29, 1859, "Education," pp. 1–3.

23. *Ibid.*; and *Proceedings of the Church Missionary Society* (1867–68), pp. 49–50.

For about twenty years African boys and girls were cared for and taught under the auspices of the Asylum. In addition to English and Bible studies, the girls received training in sewing and cooking in order to obtain employment as domestics, and the boys were trained as carpenters and masons. Some became missionaries and returned to Africa. In fact, David Livingstone sent several African boys to the school; and when he went to Nasik in 1865, eight or nine of them returned with him to Africa. One of those boys, Chuma, was with Livingstone when he died and took the body from the interior to Zanzibar and on to England. Some of the others at Nasik helped to establish missions in East Africa. The example of Mathew Wellington at Freretown has already been cited. William Benjamin left Nasik to start a mission in Mozambique.[24]

In February, 1859, there were fifty-one Africans enrolled in the Asylum, but for unexplained reasons some had left. Two boys, eighteen and nineteen years old, had enrolled in a Robert Money school and were preparing to become ministers for other Africans. There is no record of the others. Freed African girls, not from Nasik, were enrolled in the orphanage of a Mr. Jerome of the CMS. Other Abyssinian and Somali girls were taken to other schools where they were taught reading, writing, and Bible studies. In addition, they were taught the Hindustani or Marathi languages, and it was noted that they had the good "musical talent of the African race." It is not clear what the relationship was between these schools, except they were all sponsored by the CMS and seem to have shared some teachers.[25]

In 1874 the Asylum was closed, and the African students were sent as missionaries to Mombasa. This reflected the efforts on the part of the English government and missionaries to establish communities of freedmen on the African coast. This had been strongly recommended by David Livingstone in the 1860s and by Sir Bartle Frere

24. Bombay, Home Department, April 29, 1859, "Education," pp. 1–3; *Proceedings of the CMS*, pp. 49–50, 82; Bombay, *Gazetteer of the Bombay Presidency, Kolaba and Janjira* (Bombay, 1883), XIV, 87; and Elizabeth G. K. Hewat, *Christ and Western India: A Study of the Growth of the Indian Church in Bombay City from 1813* (Bombay, 1953), pp. 195–97.

25. Bombay, Home Department, April 29, 1859, "Education," R. E. Cousins (Assistant Minister of Trinity Chapel and Superintendent of the African Asylum) to H.D., February 15, 1859, pp. 1–3.

in his report of 1873. But by this time, twenty years after the Asylum had been established, more than 200 Africans had attended the school, and several of them had become part of the Nasik community. They worked as laborers on the railroad and in a variety of menial jobs. Over the next few years observers noted that the slums of Nasik were made up of Africans.[26] Although the African presence is still visible in Nasik, it has obviously fused with other racial elements. There are no figures to indicate the size of the Afro-Indian element there.

Aden, Bombay, and Nasik are only three of the provinces of freedom for Africans liberated in Asia. It is unfortunate that so little information is available about these communities, for it seems clear that the pattern of manumission and the subsequent adjustments of Africans and their descendants in Asia paralleled in many ways those better-known developments in the Western hemisphere. Perhaps further research will bring these points into clearer focus and help us to understand some of these peculiar and complex aspects of African bondage in Asia.

26. *Annual Report of the Church Missionary Society* (Bombay, 1872), pp. 10–11.

6.

Africans
in Asian History

THERE ARE virtually no published materials available in English or French about African communities in Iran, and I was unable to find an Iranian who knew of any such study in Arabic or Persian. However, Professor E. Bastani-Parizi of the University of Tehran has written several histories of Iran in which he briefly mentions African slaves and small settlements of African descendants. Some of the towns and villages he refers to are Zanjiabad ("village built by Africans"), Gala-Zanjian ("castle of Africans") in Baluchistan near a mountain called Mount of the Blacks, and Deh-Zanjian ("village of Africans") in Kerman Province.[1]

In Jiruft, an interior Persian entrepôt which relied on commerce with Hormuz, Minab, and Bandar Abbas, merchants from India, Ethiopia, East Africa generally, the Roman Empire, and other areas conducted a substantial trade which included African slaves. It is very likely that the inhabitants of the separate, black community near Jiruft are descendants of those African merchants and slaves. The inhabitants recall an African background and slavery and are sensitive to the suspicion with which they are regarded by other Iranians. Their general isolation has contributed to their dialect, which most other Iranians seem not to understand and which in part accounts for their "strangeness." There is another black community

---

1. E. Bastani-Parizi, *Tarikh-e-Kerman* (Tehran, 1961), pp. 307, 476, translated for the author by Professor Boheni, English Department, University of Tehran, in September, 1967.

near the port of Bandar Abbas, and it seems to be composed of the descendants of African slaves who worked as dhow crewmen and laborers on nearby date plantations. Also, many of the present residents of Shiraz recall reports of African men and women slaves accompanying Iranian Muslims from the Hadj, but no separate African community seems to exist in Shiraz today. Additional evidence of the African presence in Iran is the fact that the mother of the esteemed poet, Abu l'Makarim Mujir al Din, born in 1197, was an Ethiopian.[2] Very likely there are other cases of an African presence in Iran because so many sources refer to African slaves along the northern Persian Gulf, but this story must await additional research.

Although writers in India during the Middle Ages do not seem to have investigated the African origins of the Habshis, from time to time they refer to a unique or outstanding African in a particular Indian community. One of the earliest examples occurred in the thirteenth century, when it was reported that Queen Raziya, the sovereign of the sultanate of Delhi, became attracted to a Habshi slave named Jalal-ud-din Yaqut, whom she appointed to the post of royal stable master. There is no description of Yaqut's African background or the experiences he had en route to India. However, the noted Arab historian Ferista wrote that "a very great degree of familiarity was observed to exist between the Abyssinian and the Queen." They became so intimate that Yaqut would assist her onto her horse "by raising her up under the arms." The queen's father and the nobles not only protested that kind of behavior, but they later killed Yaqut.[3]

Another African in Delhi was Malik Sarvar, whom R. C. Majumdar describes as a eunuch, probably of "Negro" blood. He was a slave of Sultan Muhammad and in 1389 became the sultan's deputy, with the title of Khvaja Jahan. The sultan later conferred on him the title of Malik-ush-Sharq ("chief of the east") and appointed him gover-

2. Bastani-Parizi, *History of the Saljuks and Goz in Kerman* (Tehran, 1964), pp. 12, 13, 15, 62, 176; and the oral testimonies of some United States Peace Corps Volunteers, Iranian professors at the University of Tehran and Paklovi University in Shiraz, and civil servants and merchants in Tehran, Isfahan, Shiraz, and Bandar Abbas during 1967.

3. Quoted in John Briggs, *History of the Rise of the Mohamedan Power in India* (London, 1829), I, 220.

nor of the eastern province. Malik-ush-Sharq left Delhi for Jaunpur in 1394 and eventually began to rule as an independent king. He was later succeeded by an adopted son whose name was Malik Qaranful ("clove"), a name commonly given to African slaves. Some observers assume, therefore, that he was African. His official title was Sultan Mubarak Shah. The next king in this line was Mubarak's brother, Ibrahim, who ascended to the throne as Shams-ud-din Ibrahim. His identity is more obscure. If he were in fact Mubarak's brother, he was probably African. Majumdar simply states that after Mubarak died in 1402, "the amirs raised his brother Ibrahim to the throne." The lack of a clearer identification of Ibrahim is most unfortunate, because it was during his rule that Jaunpur became famous and prosperous. It emerged as a center of learning, attracting renowned writers; it is also noted for its impressive architecture, especially the mosques. But whatever the ethnic identity of Ibrahim, it is likely that both Malik-ush-Sharq and Mudbarak Shah were Africans. The three together made Jaunpur a prominent kingdom during the fifteenth century.[4]

During the second half of the fifteenth century, Africans in another part of northern India, Bengal, organized and asserted considerable political power. Rukn-ud-din Barbak, king of Bengal (1459–74) is said to have been the first Indian king to promote substantial numbers of African slaves to high rank. He maintained an estimated 8,000 African slave-soldiers in his army. In 1481 Barbak was succeeded by his son, who in turn was succeeded by his son. The last-named was deposed in favor of an uncle, Jalal-ud-din Fath Shah, who subsequently incurred the hostility of the African slave-soldiers. Thus, in 1486 a eunuch named Sultan Shahzada, commander of the palace guards, led the Africans in a successful usurpation of power, killed Fath Shah, and assumed the throne under the title of Barbak Shah. However, an African who was loyal to Fath Shah and was commander of the army, Amir-ul-Umara Malik Andil (Indil Khan), later murdered Barbak. At the request of Fath Shah's widow he ascended to the throne under the title of Saif-ud-din Firuz. Some historians report

4. R. C. Majumdar, *The History and Culture of the Indian People: The Delhi Sultanate* (Bombay, 1960), pp. 186–87, 188, 698–702; and *The Cambridge History of India* (London, 1937), III, 251–52.

that henceforth it became the rule in Bengal that he who killed the king's assassin had a right to the throne. In any case, Firuz's three-year reign restored a measure of discipline to the army and peace to the kingdom. When he died, Nasr-ud-din Mahmud, a minor whose ancestry remains in dispute, became king. Habesh Khan, another African, became Mahmud's regent.[5] When Habesh Khan assumed dictatorial power, Sidi Badr, an African guardsman, seized the throne in 1490. He ruled for over three years, under the title of Shams-ud-din Abu Nasr Muzaffar Shah. His army of 30,000 reportedly included 5,000 Abyssinians. After his assassination in 1493, the Africans in high posts were dismissed and expelled from the kingdom. This marked the end of the African dynasty in Bengal.[6]

The Siddis of Janjira

Janjira is said to be the Marathi corruption of the Arabic word *Jazira*, which means island. It is located off the west coast of India, about 45 miles south of Bombay. The first census of Janjira Island was taken in 1872 and reported a population of 1,700, of whom 258 were Siddis. Mostly relatives of the nawab (king), they were the principal landowners and civil servants and constituted the largest Muslim group on the island. Other religious groups included Hindus, Jews, and Christians. Until the British gained control of the island in 1879, a council of Siddi nobles chose the nawab, who was the head of state and religion (Islam). After consultation with the council, the nawab could appoint and dismiss state and religious officials.[7] How the Siddis obtained, preserved, and extended their power in Janjira and on the Konkan coast, just opposite the island, is explained largely by the role Janjira played in international trade.

In ancient times Janjira, the area around Bombay, and the Kon-

5. Some observers believe Habesh Khan was Firuz's son, in which case he would have been African; others believe he was Fath Shah's son, in which case he would not have been African. See Majumdar, *History and Culture of the Indian People*, pp. 214, 215.

6. R. C. Majumdar, *An Advanced History of India* (London, 1950), pp. 345–346; and *Cambridge History of India*, III, 268–71.

7. Bombay, *Gazetteer of the Bombay Presidency, Kolaba and Janjira* (Bombay, 1883), XI, 409–23; and oral accounts.

kan coast participated in the profitable trade with Africa and Arabia. Pliny referred to the area as "the most frequented place on the pirate coast." One Indian writer, D. R. Banaji, has written that in ancient times "Siddis came to India only for the purpose of trade." Although there is very little evidence to confirm Banaji's statement, it is entirely possible that the ancient trade discussed in the Periplus did carry Africans to India's west coast. By the ninth century slaves are mentioned as being sent from the East African port of Sofala to ports in western India.[8]

According to one tradition, the Siddis arrived on Janjira Island around 1489, when an Abyssinian in the service of the nizam (king) of Ahmadnagar disguised himself as a merchant and took 300 boxes of merchandise to the island. The "merchandise" included Siddi soldiers, who on command took possession of the island, appointed one of themselves king, and thus laid the foundation for the dynasties of the Siddi nawabs. The presence of Africans on Janjira prior to this time, however, can to a large extent be traced to the East African slave trade.

From about 1530 the Portuguese developed political and economic control over parts of the west coast of India, especially the Konkan coast, where many African slaves were imported. The number of slaves imported at any one time was small — between six and ten — but their arrival was fairly continuous to about 1740, when Portuguese maritime dominance was seriously challenged by the French and British. For the most part the slaves were from Mozambique, although the Portuguese also seized African slaves when they defeated the Muscat Arabs in Diu in 1670. The slaves were generally used by the Portuguese in businesses, on farms, in domestic positions, and in other menial jobs. Some of them were trained to be priests and teachers for religious schools, especially in Goa, which became Portugal's headquarters for its East African and Asian colonies.[9]

8. D. R. Banaji, *Bombay and the Siddis* (Bombay, 1932), pp. x–xx; India, *Imperial Gazetteer of India, Bombay Presidency* (Calcutta, 1909), II, 488; and Dean Vincent, *Commerce and Navigation of the Ancients* (London, 1807), II, 157. I have been unable to establish any connection between the Siddis of Janjira and Janjero in Ethiopia.

9. The Portuguese dispatched several military missions from Goa to East Africa. At least one African, Yusuf, son of Sultan Hasan of Mombasa, was edu-

By the middle of the eighteenth century, therefore, Africans had established a long residence along India's west coast. Several observers noted the presence in this area of Abyssinian slaves, also known as Habshi Kafirs, with black skin and woolly hair.[10]

The most salient characteristic in the history of the Siddis of Janjira is the role they played from 1616 to about 1760 as prominent and successful naval guardians of the northwestern coast of India. When Malik Ambar, the African regent-minister in the Deccan, recovered the Konkan from the Mughuls in 1616, he appointed Siddi Ahmad Khan to command the area. From that point the Siddi seamen became a primary force on the Indian west coast. Malik Ambar did not exercise political or military control over Janjira; indeed, he recognized the Siddis' sea power and promised to direct trade to them in exchange for their refusal to ally themselves with the Mughuls.[11]

During the first half of the seventeenth century, British trade in the Arabian Sea increased to the point where the British East India Company sought to establish forts to protect and secure shelter for its company ships. As early as 1621 Malik Ambar attacked and inflicted a heavy loss on a British caravan.[12] The company thereupon sent Robert Jeffries to discuss the matter with Ambar, but the mission failed to gain either compensation or a promise of friendship. When subsequent negotiations with Ambar failed, the Siddis were tempted by bribes and subjected to force by company officials trying to separate the island from alliances with coastal rulers: "If wee cannot fairly obtaine it [Janjira], wee may forcibly" do so by considering Siddi interference with British shipping as piracy.[13]

This period was also marked by Mughul success in Gujarat. By 1636 Mughul armies had defeated the Marathas at Ahmadnagar, thereby becoming more dependent on an alliance with the Siddis of

---

cated in Goa by the Portuguese, who installed him on his father's throne under the name of Don Jeronimo Chingula. This is a subject on which a good deal of additional research can be done, especially in the largely unused archives in Goa.

10. Bombay, *Gazetteer, Kolaba and Janjira*, p. 433.

11. *Ibid.*, p. 434; R. V. Ramdas, "Relations between the Marathas and the Siddis of Janjira" (Ph.D. diss., University of Bombay, n.d.), p. 41.

12. William Foster, *English Factories in India, 1655–60* (Oxford, 1906), p. 208.

13. *Ibid.*, p. 331.

Janjira. (The Siddi agreement with Malik Ambar had terminated with his death in 1626.) As one Indian scholar has written:

> It is only when the Siddis of Janjira offered their services to the Moghals against the Maratha power on the sea that Aurangazib [the Mughul emperor] gave half hearted recognition to a fleet being organized on a reasonable scale. During 200 years of Moghal greatness, the Indian Sea was under alien control.[14]

The Mughuls recognized their need for a fleet in the Indian Ocean to divert the Maratha armies, to protect the Muslim pilgrims against attacks, and to guarantee the flow of trade into Mughul ports. They therefore agreed to subsidize the Janjira navy in order to achieve those objectives.[15]

From the middle of the seventeenth century, the power of the Marathas on the Konkan coast became a formidable force against Janjira. This was the time of the great Maratha hero, Shivaji, whose greatest achievement, according to one Indian military historian, was

> the welding of the Marathas into a nation . . . and he achieved this in the teeth of the opposition of four mighty Powers like the Mughul empire, Bijapur [another Indian kingdom], Portuguese India, and the Abyssinians of Janjira.[16]

Of these several foes, the Siddis of Janjira were the most persistent and obdurate. Shivaji recognized the importance of allying his forces with or reducing the power of the Siddis. When he failed to do either, Shivaji created a strong navy to guarantee the flow of trade to his kingdom and to protect his subjects from periodic raids by the Siddis, who were regarded as "pirates alien by race, creed, and language." But the great Shivaji, in spite of long and gallant attacks on Janjira, never succeeded in capturing the island, which because of its impregnability came to be known as "the rock."[17]

14. K. M. Panikkar, *India and the Indian Ocean* (London, 1945), p. 8.

15. M. S. Commissariat, *A History of Gujarat* (Calcutta, 1957), II, 173.

16. Jadunath Sarkar, *History of Aurangzib* (Calcutta, 1919), IV, 237–38. Note that Janjira is regarded as a "mighty Power."

17. Jadunath Sarkar, *Shivaji and His Times* (Calcutta, 1920), p. 251; and Mountstuart Elphinstone, *History of India* (London, 1905), pp. 549–55.

The second half of the seventeenth century was also a time of great international rivalry in western India. There were conflicts between the Mughuls and the Marathas, and between both of them and the English, the Portuguese, and the Dutch, the last three of whom were competing for political and economic spheres of influence in western India as well as in East Africa. In 1665 the Portuguese ceded Bombay to the British government, which in 1668 transferred it to the East India Company; Janjira then became vital to the company as a base for protecting its maritime vessels. Attempting to exploit this situation, the Dutch in 1673 promised ships to the Marathas if they would attack Janjira and forestall British efforts to establish a base there, but the Marathas refused the offer.[18]

The Siddis were feared all along the western coast because of their frequent, indiscriminate raids on Indian and European vessels and towns. The only force capable of challenging them was the British, but they were reluctant to antagonize the Mughuls, with whom political and economic ties were regarded as necessary. But after a disagreement with the Mughuls in 1689, the British began capturing Siddi vessels supplying Mughul armies with provisions. Commander Siddi Kasim wrote several letters demanding that the English return the vessels; when that approach failed, he landed Siddi troops near Bombay, plundered the area, and then withdrew to Janjira.[19]

From the middle of the seventeenth century, when Mughul influence was dominant, Tegbakt, ruler of Surat, had acted as Mughul agent subsidizing the Siddi navy. Early in the eighteenth century, however, the Mughuls in Delhi began losing influence in Surat because of the increased flow of British money and arms to Tegbakt. The British hoped to persuade Tegbakt to transfer the subsidy from the Siddis to them. However, Tegbakt refused the appeal; he was suspicious of the British, whom he feared more than the Siddis. Thus rebuffed, the British sought agreements with Janjira. They succeeded in negotiating a treaty of alliance and friendship in 1733. The main articles of the treaty stipulated that, in case of war, Britain was to

18. Banaji, *Bombay and the Siddis*, pp. 13–17.

19. Alexander Hamilton, *A New Account of the East Indies* (Edinburgh, 1927), I, 220–28; and J. A. Ovington, *Voyage to Surat in the Year 1689*, ed. H. G. Hawlinson (Oxford, 1929), p. 151.

be the chief power (because of its greater resources and experience) ; if Bombay were attacked, Janjira was to contribute thirty small fighting boats and 2,000 troops; if Janjira were attacked, Britain was to supply marines from Bombay. The two powers agreed to join against their enemies, and the consent of both governments was required for any peace settlements. The following year the East India Company agreed to subsidize the Janjira fleet as a further inducement to prevent them from aligning with "other forces hostile to English interests."[20]

Meanwhile, the Dutch continued their efforts to win Siddi support. They sought the cooperation of the Surat ruler and the Siddi fleet commander in an effort to secure a commercial monopoly at Surat. The fleet commander, Siddi Masud, seems to have cooperated with them, in spite of the treaty between Britain and Janjira. Although the details are not clear, between 1752 and 1756 Masud gained control of Surat with Dutch financial support; but when he was unable to maintain his control, the Dutch withdrew their aid, and control reverted to the Surat rulers.

In 1759 the British decided to eliminate Siddi influence in Surat completely. On February 15, 1759, they dispatched a large force of Europeans and Indians and several armed vessels of the East India Company's marine. On March 4, the battle ended, with the British in command of Surat. The East India Company received a promise of the fleet subsidy which Surat rulers had been paying to the Siddis. Defeated, the Siddis were allowed to return to Janjira.[21]

Over the next century the influence of the Janjira Siddis declined perceptibly. Britain's political and economic stakes in India had risen to the point where she could not allow even the more powerful European countries to interfere; without a doubt, Siddi influence had to be eliminated. The defeat of the Siddis in 1759 represented the first and most important step in that direction. During the next three-quarters of a century the Janjira navy decreased to only a shadow

20. Bombay, *Public Department Diary*, no. 5 (1732–33), no. 8 (1734–35), no. 33 (1759) ; and Bombay, *Surat Factory Diary* (March, 1735–February, 1736).

21. C. V. Aitchison, *Collection of Treaties, Engagements and Sunnuds* (London, 1876), IV, 485–87; Bombay, *Gazetteer, Kolaba and Janjira*, pp. 445–46; India, *Imperial Gazetteer, Bombay Presidency*, pp. 126–27; and Commissariat, *History of Gujarat*, p. 172.

of its earlier size and power. Then in 1834 the British government declared the island subject to British power; and later, in 1869, the first British resident officer was sent to Janjira. Although civil jurisdiction remained in Siddi hands, the resident officer had the power of review, and the Bombay government had veto power over the nawab's administration. In 1870 the nawab appealed for the return of Siddi authority; the Bombay government agreed to restore the nawab's authority if he would agree to reform his administration on the advice of the resident officer, defray all expenses of the British resident, maintain an efficient police force at a strength approved by the British, and formulate a code for revenue collection that would meet British approval. Preferential treatment of British trade was granted by the nawab, and in 1876 a British steamer began to sail between Bombay and Janjira. The final stroke against Siddi power in Janjira occurred when Siddi Ibrahim Khan died in 1879 and the British placed Siddi Ahmed Khan on the throne. There was much opposition from the Siddis, who felt that this action violated an important tradition. The great Siddi, Yacoot Khan, proclaimed on his deathbed that his family and Siddi nobles should choose a successor from among themselves. Therefore, although the Siddis were all equal candidates, it was their decision alone to choose a nawab. The action of the British denied them that prerogative and left no doubt about who the real power was in Janjira.[22] Today the Siddis' power and influence remain insignificant, though a Siddi is the ceremonial head of the island, which is a district in India.

Considering how small the Siddis were in number, their influence on Indian history is remarkable. It is unclear how they were able to wield such power over the several indigenous groups of the area. However, this was a region where Islam had been influential for centuries; and very likely it was this factor, along with the Siddis' maritime and military skills, that accounted for their success. It is no mean achievement that such a small, alien group exercised so much influence on the policies and actions of three European powers — England, Portugal, and the Netherlands — as well as local Indian

22. Bombay, Political Department, November, 1870, sec. A, pp. 121–27; *ibid.*, September, 1871, sec. A, pp. 9–25; *ibid.*, July, 1870, sec. A, pp. 234–38; Aitchison, *Treaties*, pp. 329–30; and Bombay, *Gazetteer, Kolaba and Janjira*, pp. 449–52.

powers. Furthermore, they achieved such a position without the advantage of a rich economy. Palm groves, salt, fish, timber, and some rice were the principal resources; and of those, only timber was in significant demand for export. The greatness of Janjira and the Siddis rested primarily on their strategic location in the Indian Ocean at a time when European maritime trade began to extend to South and East Asia, with India as a rich and crucial link. This phenomenon brought about European rivalry and, ultimately, British control.

Gujarat

Tradition holds that Africans were important in Gujarati armies as early as the thirteenth century, but it is likely that there were African mercenaries and slaves in Gujarat even earlier. However, by the sixteenth century Africans not only played significant roles in the armies but also rose to political and economic power. Although some of them no doubt descended from early African settlers in the region, many were also descendants of slaves and of Abyssinian prisoners taken by Arabs during the Muslim invasion of Ethiopia in 1527. Some of the latter were brought to Gujarat in 1531 by Mustafa bin-Bahram, a Turkish commander who was ordered by Constantinople to help defend Muslim India against Portugal. Mustafa's forces included Abyssinian prisoners, some of whom remained in Gujarat as merchants and mercenary soldiers. This seems to have been a principal base from which the subsequent Gujarati Habshi community emerged.[23]

There were several Habshis of particular note in the sixteenth century. When Mandal Dilawar Khan, a captain of Arab troops in Gujarat, was killed in battle in 1553, his deputy, an African named Yacut Sabit Khan Habshi, succeeded him as commander and received the honorary title of Ulugh Khan. Yacut was in turn succeeded by his son Khayrat Khan, who received the same honorary title and became a noted military commander. He was a patron of Hajji-ad-Dabir, a prominent author who wrote an Arabic history of Gujarat. Another

23. Commissariat, *History of Gujarat*, p. 470.

Abyssinian, Jhujhar Khan, son of an earlier Habshi noble, was a commander who died in a battle near Diu in 1546 while protecting Gujarat from the Portuguese.[24]

In 1572 one of the important African nobles of Gujarat was Ikhtiyar-ul-Mulk, a commander of Habshi guards. Although he paid homage to the Mughul emperor, Akbar, he deserted with his troops and rallied Afghans, Gujaratis, Rajputs, and Habshis in rebellion against Akbar. His rebel force eventually numbered about 20,000; although finally defeated by Akbar, he commanded the respect of Mughuls and Gujaratis alike.[25]

Sheik Sayeed al-Habshi Sultani was originally a Habshi slave who became a mercenary soldier. On the death of his master, Mahmud III, around 1530, he joined Jhujhar Khan's army and served many years as a distinguished soldier. When he retired, he acquired some land and became a wealthy noble, accumulating a large library which attracted scholars. He is said to have owned many horses, camels, and slaves. After having performed the Hadj, he became well respected, giving alms to the poor and feeding an estimated 1,000 people daily.[26]

In 1573, just three years before his death, Sayeed (Sa'id) constructed a mosque in Ahmadabad. The chronogram for its construction reads: "For the sake of Allah he erected this mosque, and the builder is Sa'id." Known as Siddi Sa'id's mosque, it is simple in design with a roof built of arches. Its most beautiful features are the arched perforated windows with exquisite tracery and floral designs.[27] James Fergusson, noted authority on Indian and Eastern architecture, has observed of this mosque:

> It would be difficult to excel the skill with which the vegetable forms are conventionalized just to the extent required for the purpose . . . but perhaps the greatest skill is shown in the even manner in which the pattern is spread over the whole surface. There are some ex-

24. *Ibid.*, p. 471.

25. *Ibid.*, pp. 508–24, 441–43, 448.

26. E. Dension Ross, *An Arabic History of Gujarat* (London, 1921), II, 640–43.

27. Ratnamanirao B. Jhote, *Ahmadabad* (n.p., n.d.) p. 16.

quisite specimens of tracery in precious marbles at Agra and Delhi, but none quite equal to this.[28]

The same expert, together with a colleague, wrote:

It is probably more like a work of nature than any other architectural detail that has been designed, even by the best architects of Greece or of the Middle Ages.[29]

Although the British colonials used the mosque for offices, British Consul Lord Curzon had it set aside as a monument. Today it occupies a square in the center of Ahmadabad. Commissariat wrote: "This lovely and world-famous mosque is the last noble specimen of the great creative period of the Muslim architecture of Gujarat."[30]

Siddi Bashire also built a mosque in Ahmadabad. The story behind this mosque is obscure. However, it is unique in that it has two shaking minarets, each comprising three stories. When one minaret is shaken, the vibration is carried to the other by the roof which joins them. Echoes are similarly carried from one to the other. This style is reported to have been an innovation at the time.[31]

The following lesser-known Africans are credited with constructing buildings and aqueducts in the vicinity of Ahmadabad: Ikhtiyar Khan, Oasim Khan, and Siddi Shamshir Khan, who were in the court of Ahmed Nizam Shah. There is also limited documentation to support oral accounts that the ruling family in the former state of Sachin was of African ancestry. In Surat, Jaffer Yab Khan, an Abyssinian slave in the family of the nawab, figured prominently in the 1758–59 invasion by the British, which ended in the restoration of Mecah [Atchund?] to the nawabship and the surrender of the castle at Surat to the English. For his participation on the side of the English, Jaffer's descendants received a pension from the British government.[32]

28. James Fergusson, *History of Indian and Eastern Architecture*, ed. James Burgess (Delhi, 1967), pp. 236–37.

29. James Fergusson and Theodore Hope, *Architecture of Ahmadabad* (London, 1866), pp. 86–87.

30. Commissariat, *History of Gujarat*, p. 505.

31. *Indian Express* (Bombay), February 2, 1968.

32. Radhey Shyam, *The Kingdom of Ahmadnagar* (New Delhi, 1966), p. 372;

Richard Burton, who traveled extensively in Gujarat during the nineteenth century, reported that 600 to 700 Africans arrived there annually. He also observed "several thousands" of African women inhabiting the region. In 1839 he saw a great number of African descendants in Karachi. "We meet them everywhere with huge water-skins on their backs, or carrying burdens fit for buffaloes." Unfortunately, Burton's curiosity did not lead him to investigate the background of this African presence in either of his studies.[33]

There are many persons of African descent in Gujarat's Gir forest and in Cutch. The proximity of this region to the Muslim provinces of Persia facilitated the migration of Africans from the Persian Gulf, where they had served as seamen and slaves. In fact, it is frequently said that Afro-Indians in western Gujarat are descendants of escaped slaves.

Whatever their origins, Africans in Gujarat played significant roles, not only in political and military matters, but also in cultural affairs. Gujarat was very likely a gateway to India for many Africans from Muslim Persia, who brought with them cultural influences from the Persian Empire. This would account for the Muslim influences — dress, names, religious ceremonies, and architecture — evident in Afro-Indian communities in this part of India today.

Bombay, Foreign Department, April 27, 1855, pp. 37–40; India, Internal Department, December, 1907, sec. B, p. 217.

33. Richard F. Burton, *Sindh and the Races That Inhabit the Valley of the Indus* (London, 1851), pp. 253, 254, 256.

7.

Malik Ambar:
African Regent-Minister
in India

THE MOST DRAMATIC assertion of power by a single African in Indian history was made by Malik Ambar, one of the great men of the Deccan, at a time when the Mughuls were extending their authority into central India. Ambar, whose original name was Shambu, was born around 1550 in Harar, a province of Ethiopia. Almost nothing is known of his life in Ethiopia, except that he was sold into slavery. The circumstances of that sale are also unknown, but it is clear that before he finally reached India he was sold several times in the Arab world — in the Hejaz, Mocha, and Baghdad, among other places.

Ambar's Rise
to Power

His master at Mocha, Kazi Hussein, recognizing that Shambu possessed intellectual qualities, thus educated him in administration and finance. It was during this period that Shambu became a Muslim and was named Ambar by Hussein.[1] When Hussein died, Ambar

1. Sheikh Chand, *Malik Ambar* (Hyderabad, 1931), pp. 1–2, translated from Urdu for the author by Marzeur Rahman, Assistant, University of Bombay Library; and D. R. Seth, "The Life and Times of Malik Ambar," *Islamic Culture: An English Quarterly*, XXXI (Hyderabad, January, 1957), 142.

91

was sold to a slave dealer, who took him to India. Around 1575 he was purchased by Chingiz Khan, the prime minister to Nizam mul-Mulk Bani, king of Ahmadnagar. Chingiz Khan was himself of African origin and may very well have been a descendant of African mercenaries who served as far back as the thirteenth century in many parts of India, especially in Gujarat, where Ahmadnagar is located. At any rate, in the late sixteenth century, Chingiz Khan was one of several prominent Habshis in the area. When Khwanze Humayun, the queen of Ahmadnagar, sought to consolidate her power after her husband's death, her son Murtaza I led several Habshis in a successful revolt in which the queen was imprisoned. Chingiz Khan continued as prime minister.[2]

Chingiz Khan was impressed by Ambar's knowledge of Arabic, his loyalty, and his general intelligence. It is likely that those qualities also won Ambar the respect of other Habshi slaves. For that reason the prime minister, hoping to solidify his control of the African slave-soldiers, promoted Ambar to a position of military and administrative responsibility. With the death of the prime minister, however, Ahmadnagar became the scene of civil strife. Ambar was sold to the shah of Golconda and later to the king of Bijapur (both of these kingdoms were in the Deccan). Because of the training he had received from Kazi Hussein and Chingiz Khan, Ambar made a good impression on the king of Bijapur, who gave him the title of Malik ("like a king"). At Bijapur he became a military commander and was well respected by the Arab troops he commanded. In fact, he made it a practice to appoint Arabs to positions of command. In about 1590, when the king refused to grant him additional funds for Arab trainees, he deserted and took several Arabs with him.[3]

Malik Ambar and his Arab supporter attracted other men, both African and Deccani, and eventually built up an independent army of over 1,500 cavalrymen and infantrymen who fought as mercenaries for various kings. Thus, when the king of Ahmadnagar organized a Habshi army in 1595, the prime minister, Abhangar Khan, another

2. Bena Rasi Prasad Saksena, "Malik Ambar," *Hindustani Academy*, no. 4 (October, 1933), p. 343, translated from Hindi for the author by Shri Parnlakar, Senior Assistant, University of Bombay Library; and Chand, *Malik Ambar*, p. 5.

3. Chand, *Malik Ambar*, pp. 8–12, 14.

Habshi, invited Ambar and his men to join him.[4] This return to Ahmadnagar provided the opportunity for Ambar to become a great champion of the Deccanis against the Mughuls. Ambar and a Deccani, Mian Raju Dakhani, combined their military efforts on several occasions to repel attacks by the Mughuls. Although they eventually became political and military rivals, Raju and Ambar fought together gallantly to defend their province.[5]

Ambar and Raju were able and popular rivals; they were also ambitious, and each sought to gain control over King Murtaza II. In 1602 Ambar imprisoned Murtaza and named himself regent-minister. He resisted several Mughul attacks and prevented the Great Mughul, Emperor Akbar, from fulfilling his aim of conquering the Deccan. By the time Jahangir succeeded Akbar in 1605, Ambar had founded a capital at Kirkee and had become well entrenched in the Deccan. He continued to fight off his rival, Raju; in 1607 he captured him and had him executed. Ambar thus stood supreme in Ahmadnagar.[6]

Ambar organized an estimated 60,000-horse army. His light cavalry was very effective as a mobile unit; he also employed artillery obtained from the British. Ambar also enlisted the naval support of the Siddis of Janjira in 1616 in order to cut Mughul supply lines and in general to conduct harassing missions.[7] His guerrilla tactics were particularly successful. On one occasion Emperor Jahangir observed:

> Ambar the black-faced, who had himself in command of the enemy, continually brought up reinforcements till he assembled a large force. . . . It was deemed expedient to retreat and prepare for a new campaign.[8]

4. Ibid., pp. 15–17; Saksena, "Malik Ambar," pp. 342–48.

5. Bombay, *Gazetteer of the Bombay Presidency, Ahmadnagar* (Bombay, 1884), XVII, 389.

6. Seth, "Life and Times," pp. 145, 146, 147; and Bombay, *Gazetteer, Ahmadnagar*, p. 390. According to one source, Kirkee "was not only the best city in the Deccan, but the like of it was not found even in Hindustan" (*Lalit Kala: A Journal of Oriental Art, Chiefly Indian*, nos. 1, 2 [April, 1955–March, 1956], p. 24).

7. See pp. 82–83 above.

8. Quoted in J. D. B. Gribble, *A History of the Deccan* (London, 1896), I, 253–54.

This was only one of several times the Mughuls were forced to re-treat. While Ambar probably benefited from disputes between Jahan-gir and his son, which ultimately led to revolt, Ambar, too, frequently fought rivals in order to strengthen his position in the Deccan.[9]

Ambar built his greatest fortifications at Daulatabad to protect his kingdom from Prince Shah Jahan, who later became a great Mughul emperor. In 1621 Shah Jahan's forces launched an attack against Daulatabad in which they suffered heavy losses. Despite this initial victory, however, Ambar was aware that he could not withstand the Mughuls without allies. He therefore continued to seek the coopera-tion of the Deccanis; to secure the support of Ibrahim Adil Shah II, Ambar had his daughter marry the shah's favorite courtier. His long and distinguished service in Golconda and Bijapur brought support from those southern kingdoms, for they realized that Ambar served as a buffer between them and the Mughuls.

By the 1620s, however, Ambar was having difficulty in maintain-ing the loyalty of his officers. Almost continuous warfare for about twenty years had demoralized many Deccanis and had drained much from the economy of the kingdom. Although Ambar was never con-quered, he had suffered several defeats. Thus, when he died in 1626 at close to eighty years of age, friction and enmity were just be-neath the surface. His son, Fettah Khan, succeeded him as regent-minister of the kingdom; but in 1629 the nizam reduced Fettah's status to that of an officer and later imprisoned him for insubordina-tion. Thus ended the short but influential rule of Africans in the Deccan.[10]

Ambar's Achievements

Several Indian writers have favorably assessed Malik Ambar's reign. With regard to administration, his early training by Kazi Hussein and Chingiz Khan proved invaluable. He improved the com-munication system within his kingdom by developing a postal service

---

9. *Ibid.*, pp. 251, 252; and Saksena, "Malik Ambar," p. 341.

10. Bombay, *Gazetteer, Ahmadnagar*, p. 395; and Seth, "Life and Times," p. 150.

with messengers dispatched throughout the region. He recognized that the Deccan was inhabited by several minority groups whose loyalty he would receive only if they had a stake in the kingdom. He particularly encouraged the enlistment of Habshis in his army and gave them a Koranic education. Some of them became businessmen, but the largest number were enlisted in his private guard. He reportedly purchased 1,000 Habshi slaves for this guard, which became a strong corps of shock troops.[11] Ambar granted land to Hindu residents and appointed Brahmins as his principal financial officials and tax collectors. Marathas were also prominent as clerks in the military and civil service. Arabs and Habshis were appointed to key military posts; they also, along with Persians, were the core of small business. Arabs and Persians monopolized the foreign trade, principally between the Deccan and the Persian Gulf. During Ambar's reign a great amount of silk and paper were manufactured; arms — swords, axes, and guns — were also made. Those items provided a solid base for trade with various parts of India, Persia, and Arabia, and trade was also developed with the Portuguese and the English.[12]

Ambar's land policy deserves special mention. Both communal and private ownership of property were practiced. Communal property, prevalent in rural or village areas, was regarded as joint property of the people. Canals and irrigation schemes were fostered to improve trade and agriculture, and taxes levied on the use of those facilities were paid in kind to the central treasury. Lower rates of taxation were applied to the poorer areas of the kingdom and even to the richer districts when there were crop failures. Private land ownership was fostered in the more prosperous districts in order to encourage greater production through competition. This system, according to oral and written accounts, continued in the area until about 1822.[13]

Asad Beg, a Mughul envoy who was sent to win Ambar's favor with gifts, observed that the Habshi

11. Seth, "Life and Times," p. 155; and Chand, *Malik Ambar*, pp. 123–24.

12. Radhey Shyam, *The Kingdom of Ahmadnagar* (New Delhi, 1966), p. 280; Bombay, *Gazetteer, Ahmadnagar*, pp. 393–95; and Chand, *Malik Ambar*, pp. 123–29, 185–87, 190–91, 195.

13. Bombay, *Gazetteer, Ahmadnagar*, pp. 323–24, 393–95; and Chand, *Malik Ambar*, pp. 127, 154–58.

was a fairly cultured man loving the society of the learned and the pious. He was also very punctilious in the observance of the routine of religion. . . . He became the nucleus of the revival of the cultural traditions of Ahmadnagar.[14]

An Arab historian, Shili Trimi, has written that Ambar attracted poets and scholars, mostly Arab and Persian, to the royal court and rewarded them, sometimes appointing them royal advisers. The official language of the court was Persian, though Arabic and Marathi were common languages among the general public. Ambar also patronized Hindu men of learning, and at Kirkee he built a place "where Hindus and other pundits gathered." Schools were started, and free education was available, though their extent is not known.[15] All of these cultural achievements were part of the tradition of Islam and contributed to the praise Ambar received from both Arabs and Persians: "In the service of the Prophet of God there was Bilal; after a thousand years came another, Malik Ambar."[16]

Ambar's reign is also noted for architectural developments. Long, wide roads were laid, canals and drains were built, public gardens were laid out, and several mosques and public buildings were constructed in and around Kirkee. The most renowned buildings are the Kalachabutra ("black stadium," in which elephant games were played), the Kalamajid ("black mosque"), the Bhadkal Darwaza, and the Nakhuda Mhala (royal public buildings).[17] An interesting discussion centers on the fact that Ambar's public buildings and his tomb are made of black stone. One group maintains that this was coincidental, that black stone was available in the region and would probably have been used as building material by any sovereign interested in architecture. (The fact remains, however, that other

14. Quoted in Saksena, "Malik Ambar," p. 603.

15. Seth, "Life and Times," p. 154; Chand, *Malik Ambar*, pp. 148, 194–96; and Shyam, *Ahmadnagar*, pp. 284–85.

16. Chand, *Malik Ambar*, p. 195. Bilal, an Ethiopian, was Prophet Mohammed's muezzin (caller for the Muslim prayer services).

17. See Chand, *Malik Ambar*, pp. 163–76; Shyam, *Ahmadnagar*, p. 287; Seth, "Life and Times," p. 154; Gulam Ahmad Khan, "History of the City of Aurangabad," in *Transactions of the Indian History Congress* (Hyderabad, 1941), pp. 604–5; and Bombay, *Gazetteer of the Bombay Presidency, Aurangabad* (Bombay, 1884), p. 172.

stones were available in the region, but Malik Ambar limited his buildings to the black stone.) A second group proposes that Ambar constructed the public buildings of black stone because he was sensitive about his African heritage and color. It is reported that on several occasions derogatory comments were made about his blackness. The Mughul emperor, Jahangir, associated Ambar's color with degradation and, according to some historians, seldom mentioned Ambar in his *Memoirs* without abuse.[18] While this may not have reflected racism or even a sense of cultural superiority on his part, Jahangir's comments do at least reveal a sensitivity to color which could very well have carried value judgments. One could reasonably conclude, therefore, that Ambar's desire to dignify his color, together with the availability of black stone, encouraged him to construct impressive black buildings around Kirkee.

Malik Ambar's achievements in the Deccan would have been impressive even if he had been a member of the native majority; but as a member of an immigrant minority group, which on occasion was the object of degrading epithets, Ambar's place in Deccani history must be regarded as a mark of greatness. A few historians have accorded him that honor. Elliot and Dowson wrote:

> Ambar was a slave, but an able man. In warfare, in command, in sound judgments and in administration, he had no rival or equal. . . . History records no other instance of an Abyssinian slave arriving at such eminence.[19]

Ferista, a contemporary Arab historian, regarded Ambar as one "who had risen from the condition of a slave to great influence." Ferista continues in most generous praise of the African:

> The justice and wisdom of the government of Mullik Ambar have become proverbial in the Deccan. He appears to have been the most enlightened financier of whom we read in Indian history.[20]

18. Gribble, *Deccan*, p. 252; Saksena, "Malik Ambar," p. 341; and *Lalit Kala*, p. 24.

19. H. M. Elliot and J. Dowson, *History of India As Told by Its Own Historians* (London, 1867), VI, 414–15. See also Gribble, *Deccan*, I, 256.

20. Quoted in Elliot and Dowson, *History of India*, p. 320.

D. R. Seth notes that Jahangir, the great Mughul emperor who had failed to conquer Ambar and had called him despicable names, nonetheless admired the Habshi's record. In his *Memoirs* Jahangir wrote: "In the art of soldiering Ambar was unique in his age."[21] Mirza Muhammad Hadi, who continued Jahangir's *Memoirs*, wrote:

> Ambar, whether as a commander or strategist was without an equal in military art. He kept the rabble of that country [the Deccan] in perfect order and to the end of his days lived in honour. There is no record elsewhere in history of an African slave attaining to such a position as was held by him.[22]

Seth gave Ambar highest praise when he wrote:

> Malik Ambar was one of the greatest men who played their parts on the stage of Deccan history. The Moghuls succeeded in conquering the Deccan only after his death.[23]

The noted historian of Gujarat, Radhey Shyam, characterized the twenty years of Ambar's rule: "The history of the next twenty years of the Nizam Shahi kingdom [Ahmadnagar] may be said to be a record of heroic activities of one individual [Ambar]."[24]

According to oral testimonies in Hyderabad in 1968, Malik Ambar is still regarded as a great figure in Deccani history, best remembered and most revered by the Muslims. His accomplishments unquestionably established him as an outstanding figure in Indian history. The example of Malik Ambar substantiates two important points: Africans played significant roles in Indian history, and they managed to win and maintain the support and respect of numerous Indians, primarily Muslims. The conclusion must be that Islam provided a common denominator for cultural identification and was a means of facilitating political and military success for Africans in the Deccan.

21. Quoted in Seth, "Life and Times," p. 155.
22. Quoted in *Lalit Kala*, p. 24.
23. Seth, "Life and Times," p. 142.
24. Shyam, *Ahmadnagar*, p. 329.

8.

Siddi Risala:
A Community of African Descent
in Hyderabad

SEVERAL WRITERS have referred to the existence of African slave-soldiers in southwest Asia and India during the Middle Ages, but they have not explained the nature of the African immigration, the genesis of the communities of African descent, the resultant attitudes of the indigenous and immigrant communities, or the extent of acculturation. With regard to medieval India, several of the standard histories make frequent references to the cooperation between the Africans and the Deccanis (Muslim Indians domiciled in the Deccan of India from about the eighth century), while they refer to Turks, Arabs, Persians, and Mughuls as the "foreigners or homeless." A possible reason why the Africans were not regarded as foreigners is that they had established themselves in the Deccan long before the other groups mentioned. A more plausible explanation, however, is that the Africans were Sunni Muslims, like the Deccanis, whereas most of the other immigrants were Shi'ites.[1] According to R. C. Ma-

1. For discussion of this subject, see H. M. Elliot and J. Dowson, *History of India As Told by Its Own Historians* (London, 1867); John Briggs, *History of the Rise of the Mohamedan Power in India* (London, 1829); J. D. B. Gribble, *A History of the Deccan* (London, 1896); *The Cambridge History of India* (London, 1937), Vols. III, IV; S. Lane-Poole, *The Muhammadan Dynasties* (London, 1894); Iftikhar Ahmad Ghauri, "Muslims in the Deccan — An Historical Survey," *Journal of the Research Society of Pakistan* (January, 1965). The Sunnis accept the first four successors to Mohammed as legitimate; the Shi'ites do not. Since Mohammed had no surviving son, the Shi'ites maintain that his daughter's

99

jumdar: "The *dark-skinned*, illiterate, unprepossessing Abyssinians were at a great disadvantage and were treated with contempt by the *fair* pardesis [foreigners]."[2] Perhaps racial stereotypes were manifested more among the "foreigners," thereby causing an alignment between Africans and Deccanis. These interpretations raise many questions related to African migrations to Asia from earliest times and should be the subject of more intensive research. The concern of this chapter, however, is the migration of Africans to India during the nineteenth century and the subsequent emergence of a community of African descent in Hyderabad, a central Indian city in the Deccan.

Hyderabad Province
and the Slave Trade

During the nineteenth century, African migrations to Asia in general and India in particular resulted primarily — indeed, almost exclusively — from various forms of the centuries-old East African slave trade, which had increased in intensity because of European and American as well as Asian involvement. Ironically, this was also the period of increasing British pressure on European powers, the United States, and the sultan of Zanzibar to restrict and ultimately to abolish the slave trade. But early efforts to abolish the trade had little immediate effect. The trade continued to various degrees in Cutch, Kathiawar, Diu, Bombay, Goa, the Malabar Coast, and throughout the province of Hyderabad.[3]

In 1841 an Arab merchant reported that Hyderabadi agents in Muscat were buying African slaves. In 1842 the British resident in

husband, Ali, was entitled to succeed him. These two groups have developed differences in some ceremonies and civil laws. See H. A. R. Gibb, *Mohammedanism* (London, 1949) ; and Reuben Levy, *The Social Structure of Islam* (Cambridge, Mass., 1962).

2. R. C. Majumdar, *The History and Culture of the Indian People: The Delhi Sultanate* (Bombay, 1960), p. 265 (Majumdar's italics).

3. Diu and Goa developed as slave ports under the Portuguese, who also administered Mozambique. Although the British seized and liberated African slaves on Arab dhows, they did not take such direct action against the Portuguese.

Hyderabad observed that a heavy traffic in slaves was being conducted in the city by Arabs, some of whom were mercenary soldiers.[4] In the same year the resident in the Persian Gulf, Lt. Col. H. D. Robertson, reported that many Muslim slave dealers and the chief slave markets of India were in the towns of the nizam of Hyderabad province. Some of those dealers were Habshis working with Arabs. Reuben Aslam, an Arab agent in Muscat, reported that one Yacoob, a Habshi of Jedda married to a Hyderabadi woman, was engaged in the slave trade. He brought slaves who posed as his wives and daughters into Hyderabad and sold them. The assistant resident in Hyderabad confirmed that Yacoob and an Arab, Shaik Mohamed, were well known in the city as slave dealers. Yacoob, a former slave, was known to have brought back several slaves from his visits to Arabia and to have sold them. Sometimes he purchased children from poor Indian families and sold them in Aurangabad, another Indian city. The resident observed that there were several dealers in Hyderabad and that every wealthy family there had three or four domestics purchased either from poor families or from Arab slave dealers who sold Africans in their homes. The following were listed as Arab dealers: Moobarick bin Mooullin, Laaeed bin Hameed, Houssain Rudaaee, Ali Mookaree, Ismail Fuquchee, Ahmed bin Alia Aseeree. Some of these dealers also engaged in selling Hindu girls in the Persian Gulf.[5]

In December, 1869, the British political agent in Turkish Arabia reported that many African slaves were allegedly disguised as women in order to pass by the Bombay customs officials. Female slaves and men disguised as women posed as wives and daughters of the dealers. Dr. E. G. Balfour, deputy inspector general of hospitals in Secunderabad-Hyderabad, confirmed that a number of Africans were imported into Hyderabad as domestics and that many Arabs returned from the pilgrimage to Mecca with one or two Africans who posed as members of the family. The presence of Africans in the city was also noted by the resident of Hyderabad in 1870; he rejected the term "slave," however, because he believed that the Africans could leave their "masters." He based this belief on a report by Nawab

4. Bombay, Political Department, August 3, 1842, pp. 335–36.
5. *Ibid.*

(Deputy) Sir Salar Jung, who wrote to Maj. W. Tweedie, first assistant resident of Hyderabad, that although some Arabs did bring Africans with them from Arabia, he could not confirm that the Africans were slaves because soon after their arrival they were seen working for other "masters."[6] He noted that:

> since I have assumed the administration, except for one or two cases, I have not heard of any complaint from any African of oppression having been exercised on him, or any complaint touching slavery.[7]

Although it was generally recognized that disguised African slaves were landed in Bombay, the commissioner of customs denied that such landings took place "to any extent." According to him, Africans from Arabia appeared to be satisfied members of the family and did not seem to have been brought against their will.[8]

There were also some free Africans who migrated to Hyderabad. Slaves liberated from Arab dhows were frequently landed at Bombay between the 1830s and 1875. Some of those freedmen found employment or guardians in Bombay, but others migrated to Hyderabad in search of work. There seems to be no way of determining the extent of this flow into the city, but without a doubt there was a sizable community of Africans in nineteenth-century Hyderabad.

The African Cavalry Guard

When the Hyderabad military forces became part of the British-Indian army in 1857, Sir Salar Jang I raised a regular Hyderabad army which included a group of fifty Africans in the service of the raja of Wanparthy. The raja's African troops seem to have been the continuation of a tradition which dated back to at least the Middle Ages, when Hyderabad was part of the Muslim Bahmani kingdom (1347–1512) and many African slaves fought for Bahmani princes.[9]

6. *Ibid.*, April, 1871, sec. A, pp. 40–51; and *ibid.*, August, 1870, pp. 376–77.
7. *Ibid.*, December, 1870, p. 377.
8. *Ibid.*, April, 1871, pp. 40–51.
9. The most distinguished African soldier was Malik Ambar (see Chapter 7),

Although the Deccan was finally absorbed by the Mughuls between 1626 and 1675, several Hindu rulers, including the raja of Wanparthy, retained African contingents.[10]

In 1863 the nizam of Hyderabad assumed command of the raja's African troops and organized them as the African Cavalry Guard, also known as the African Bodyguards. The ranks of the guard were increased initially by the enlistment of Africans in the Hyderabad area, but over the next few years the nizam began dispatching agents to various parts of Arabia to recruit Africans. Over the years it became customary for physically fit sons of guardsmen to become members of the guard. At an early age the boys performed menial chores in the nizam's court, in addition to receiving instruction on the loyalty and duties required of bodyguards. By 1895 the guard had expanded to 305 troopers mounted on horses and armed with sabers.[11]

During the latter part of the nineteenth century the nizam began to select young Arab and Siddi boys as khanazahs (protégés). As khanazahs, they were better fed, better dressed, and had greater freedom of mobility in Hyderabad than the other guardsmen. They also received their education at the nizam's court. Eventually, most of the khanazahs became trusted advisers of the nizam. One Siddi who became a khanazah was Nasir bin Muftah, who served for over thirty years in the guard. He began as a lineman, moved up to watchman, and ultimately became superintendent of the nizam's entire household, a post he held when the guard was disbanded in 1951. In this last capacity, one of Muftah's duties was to supervise the nizam's kitchen, which reportedly fed over 20,000 persons daily — family, concubines, servants, and nobles and their families. After having saved the nizam from an attempted assassination in 1947, Muftah became the nizam's closest confidant. He evidently was rewarded for his loyalty; today his wealth is considerable, and he owns several rental properties and a poultry farm with some 2,000 chickens. His son

---

but there is no available evidence that the Hyderabadi Siddis are his descendants or in any way related to his era.

10. India, Secret Department, February, 1895, "Correspondence and Reports Relating to the Troops of Hyderabad State" (Hyderabad Residency, September 29, 1890), pp. 1–6.

11. *Ibid.*

Hussain, also a former khanazah, owns property in Hyderabad as well.

Most Siddis, however, did not become khanazahs but were ordinary members of the guard. The guardsmen were not a fighting unit. They served as the nizam's bodyguards, supervised and maintained the court, and performed as drill teams, singers, and dancers on ceremonial occasions. Only one Siddi ever attained a rank as high as captain. The terms of service were flexible enough to allow some of the guards to hire out their services during their spare time. They were frequently called on, for example, to sing and dance for weddings and other unofficial activities.[12]

As his main fighting force the nizam had an Arab army, in which a few Africans served. This unit caused considerable concern during the 1880s, when there was apprehension that the large Arab minority in Hyderabad might, with the assistance of Arabs in Arabia, attempt to seize political control from the nizam.[13] Indeed, one of the reasons why the nizam chose Africans to be his private bodyguards was that they, unlike the Arabs, were a very small minority with a foreign culture and language and could not easily identify with any potentially dissident group in the area. But most of the Africans were Muslim, spoke some Arabic, and began to associate with members of the Arab community of Hyderabad. This relationship was facilitated by the fact that both Africans and Arabs served in the nizam's army. In addition, since few African women lived in Hyderabad (not all those who entered Hyderabad province lived in the city of Hyderabad), African men sought and were received by Arab women in marriage.

Recognizing the possibility of African cooperation in an Arab attempt to seize political control, the government of India in 1882 began to restrict the movement of Africans into Hyderabad. It justified this action by explaining that the Africans "consort with Arabs, follow the same leaders, are of the same turbulent habits, and, for police purposes, are practically the same."[14] Africans were detained at Bombay and were not allowed to proceed to Hyderabad unless they

12. India, Army Record Office (Hyderabad), "Siddi Report," p. 2.

13. India, Political Department, December, 1882, "Report on the Emigration of Siddhies into Hyderabad," I, 110–13.

14. *Ibid.*

had been provided with a pass from the resident in Aden. Presumably, he would be careful to issue passes only to individuals known to be loyal to the Indian government. Aden, in addition to being a major source of African immigrants, was also the area from which most of the Hyderabadis of Arab descent had originated and therefore the area from which most of the Arab opposition was anticipated. The restrictive measures had only limited effect on the migration of Africans to Hyderabad. Slaves could still enter, posing as wives and children of Arabs. The movement of Arabs, especially those returning from pilgrimages to Mecca, was never checked.

Both the Indians and British were fearful that the African guardsmen might secure weapons more dangerous than their sabers. According to a report by an Indian commander:

> Being loose in discipline they [the guardsmen] used to indulge in drunkness [*sic*], gambling and rowdiness. Special efforts were necessary to keep them cowed down to peace and order, as there was no arms act in Hyderabad, and they could possess all sorts of weapons like matchlocks, swords, lances, and daggers.[15]

That the British were especially sensitive and apprehensive about this issue is revealed in an unofficial exchange of memoranda between Gen. George Chesney in India and the Foreign Department:

> No one at Hyderabad would like to see breechloaders under any circumstances put into the hands of the African Guard, of whom everybody there seemed to be a good deal afraid.[16]

When the nizam took eight of the guardsmen to Delhi for an official ceremony in 1905, he armed them with carbines, bandoliers, and dummy cartridges. The officiating inspector general of the Imperial Service Troops, an Englishman, vigorously reacted to this "misuse of weapons," which he labeled a "dangerous" act. The controversy was not resolved until the resident at Hyderabad confirmed that only dummy ammunition had been issued.[17]

15. "Siddi Report," p. 2.
16. India, Secret Department, January, 1890, I, 56.
17. *Ibid.*, September, 1905, pp. 42–43.

While there does not seem to be any available register to indicate the places of origin of the African guardsmen, there is sufficient evidence to suggest that the recruits came from various parts of East Africa via Arabia. This conclusion is supported partly by the discussion in the preceding chapters of the East African slave trade to India. Additional support has come from interviews with members of the Siddi community in Hyderabad. Since the slave trade to India remained active until the end of the nineteenth century, several descendants of slaves recall stories of where their parents or grandparents came from and how they were recruited. Some of these descendants recall only that their grandparents were purchased in Arabia, but several have vague ideas that Ethiopia, Zanzibar, and Mozambique were places from which their ancestors came.

The Account of
Soliaman bin Haftoo

The strongest written proof of the guardsmen's African origin is found in the numerous reports, letters, memoranda, petitions, and written testimonies relating to the case of Soliaman bin Haftoo, a trooper in the guard who claimed he was Meshesha, son of Emperor Theodore of Ethiopia.[18] Theodore reigned from 1855 to 1868 and, in the process of unifying Ethiopia, punished his enemies severely and confiscated some church lands. He thus gained the reputation of being a tyrant. But Theodore was also eager to develop the country. He invited foreign craftsmen — for example, gunsmiths and engineers — to work in Ethiopia. In 1868, because of a misunderstanding with Queen Victoria of England, he imprisoned an English envoy. This action led to the British punitive expedition to Ethiopia in 1868. Soliaman claimed that when the British expedition invaded Magdala he was with thirty or forty Ethiopians who fled. Because his father, King Theodore, was hated by many of his subjects, Soliaman, ten

18. India, Foreign Department, October, 1882, "General," sec. B, I, 81–93. Except where otherwise indicated, the remainder of Soliaman bin Haftoo's account is based on these records.

years old at the time, was advised not to disclose his identity. Some unnamed, loyal friends led him to the coast, where he embarked on a ship which took him to Aden. After a short stay there he sailed to Bombay, where he was befriended by some Goans who were Christians like himself. However, because of language difficulties and alleged dishonesty on the part of his Goan friends, Soliaman left them after about eight months. He then became friendly with some Arabs who persuaded him to convert to Islam. It was at that time that he changed his name from Meshesha to Soliaman bin Haftoo. About a year later one of the nizam's agents recruited him in Bombay for the African guard. There he met an old man, Syed Monjut, who lived in the same Ethiopian village as he. Monjut recognized Soliaman as King Theodore's son, but agreed not to discuss the matter with anyone.

About ten years passed before Soliaman discussed his identity with anyone else; then, in 1882, he sent word to the nawab sahib of Hyderabad identifying himself and requesting permission and financial assistance to return to Ethiopia. He explained that the decision to disclose his identity and request funds resulted from a letter he had received from an Ethiopian who earlier had spent a few months in Hyderabad. According to Soliaman, the letter stated that he was wanted in Ethiopia. He seems to have given no other details about the letter except that he replied on the back of it and kept the envelope.[19] As additional support for his claim, Soliaman identified his mother as Tawabatch, the daughter of Ras Ali, king of Gondar. He said his father had a son and daughter by another wife, but that he was the only son of Tawabatch, who had died about six years prior to the British expedition. The cross-shaped scar on his head, Soliaman explained, meant that he was a Christian of noble birth.

The commander of the guard spoke highly of Soliaman's character and submitted to the first assistant resident of Hyderabad statements of several troopers who supported the petitioner. The commander stated that he thought Soliaman's claim "was not without foundation." He pointed out that references in some of the statements

19. Unfortunately, I could not find that envelope or any other reference to it.

to Baber and Hill, two officers in the British expedition to Ethiopia, lent some credibility to the case.

There were two detailed statements submitted by troopers to support Soliaman's claim. Pvt. Mahomed bin Sayeed, Second Company, Myseram Regiment, testified that about fifteen years earlier, while a dealer in Ethiopia, he saw Soliaman on two occasions riding a mule. He knew him as Meshesha, then about ten years old. After about six years in Arabia, Mahomed went to Hyderabad and joined the nizam's army, where he met and recognized Soliaman. Mahomed bin Noor, African Cavalry Guard, reported that about fifteen years earlier, when he was a translator for "Mr. Mooglar," an infantry officer serving as a magistrate, he was sent to Ethiopia to work with the commissariat of the British expedition.[20] While he was attached to Captain Hill's artillery unit, he met a group of men and a boy traveling to the coast. The boy was being advised by an Arab; and, since Mahomed bin Noor understood Arabic, he learned that the boy was King Theodore's son. About fifteen days later he saw the same boy at the seaport town of "Doolabunder." Mahomed bin Noor returned to Aden, became a sailor, and went to Bombay. From there he went to Hyderabad, where he enlisted in the nizam's Myseram Regiment and served five and a half years. He spent another five years traveling in Africa and Arabia before returning to Hyderabad and joining the guard. It was on this last occasion that he recognized Soliaman, who refused to admit his identity until almost a year later.

These statements were accompanied by two shorter ones. Sgt. Furrege bin Buckree, C Troop, African Cavalry Guard, explained that he learned of Soliaman's identity from Syed bin Rujjub. While serving under Captain Baber during the Ethiopian campaign, he added, he had seen Soliaman in Ethiopia. Mahomed bin Sayeed, trooper, Myseram Regiment, supported Soliaman's statement and expressed a willingness to testify if necessary. Several other troopers had heard about Soliaman's background but could give no supporting evidence.

Maj. W. F. Prideaux, who had served on several official missions to Ethiopia, was the British resident in Jaipur, India. Because of his knowledge and experience, therefore, he was asked by the government

20. "Mr. Mooglar" was probably Col. E. Mockler, who served in Aden and nearby areas in the late nineteenth century.

of India to give his opinion on the case. After studying the petitioner's claim, Major Prideaux decided that Soliaman was an Ethiopian by birth and that he probably had left there at an early age. This opinion was based on the fact that Soliaman's memory of the country, though blurred and somewhat indistinct, did suggest that he once knew the area well. What puzzled Prideaux was that the petitioner, on becoming a Muslim, had adopted Soliaman as a name and had also adopted the Ethiopian Christian name Haftoo (Haftu, Huftoo, Habt, Habta). Prideaux decided that "Haftoo" had actually been retained as the family name, and that Soliaman was not, therefore, a legitimate son of the king. He recalled that when the British had captured Theodore at Magdala, none of his children was alive.[21] If any heir had been alive, Prideaux thought that some captive or member of the king's court would have mentioned it. The major did acknowledge, however, that Theodore had an illegitimate son, Meshesha, who must have been at least twenty-two years old at the time Magdala was captured.[22] This would have made him thirty-five; Soliaman said he was twenty-seven. Although Prideaux said he had seen Meshesha several times in Ethiopia and would recognize him, there is no evidence that he ever met or saw Soliaman.

Major Prideaux questioned how Soliaman, without speaking any language but Amharic, could have arranged his passage and exchanged his money for rupees in order to travel to India. Prideaux also said that no Ethiopian scarified himself, as Soliaman claimed, but he did acknowledge that Ethiopians cut themselves for relief from certain ailments. He also testified that the only mark to distinguish an Ethiopian Christian from a Muslim was the *mateb*, a blue silk cord worn around the neck.

21. Prideaux was mistaken in this view. Alamayu, the king's only legitimate son, was captured and sent to England, where he died in 1879. See Hormuzd Rassam, *Narrative of the British Mission to Theodore* (London, 1869), II, 335; Richard Greenfield, *Ethiopia* (New York, 1965), pp. 83–84; and Trevener J. Holland and Henry M. Hozier, *Record of the Expedition to Abyssinia* (London, 1870), II, 105.

22. In addition to Alamayu, Theodore had three daughters and two sons, including Meshesha, who were born to women he had married without any religious ceremony; thus, according to Abyssinian canon law, they were illegitimate. See Rassam, *Mission to Theodore*, II, 336.

Major Prideaux concluded that Soliaman was one of the many Ethiopians who had fled the country after the British military expedition in 1868 and that he was merely seeking a pension from the British government. Prideaux submitted his opinion to the government of India, which, by virtue of English colonial rule in India, decided the case. Basing its decision primarily on the major's conclusions, the government ruled that it would not interfere in any way with Soliaman's movements. Nothing, however, was said about financial assistance. This decision evidently closed the case; no additional records pertaining to Soliaman seem to exist.

Prideaux's conclusion was probably correct, although some of the questions he raised can be reasonably answered. It is conceivable, for example, that the petitioner did not know his exact age. He left Ethiopia as a child and spent several years traveling and adjusting to new social conditions in Arabia and India. It is also possible that he deliberately gave a younger age to the guard. Regarding other questions raised by the major, Soliaman's escape and travel were arranged by Arabs, thereby minimizing the problems of language and the exchange of money. More to the point, however, is the testimony of Meshesha's family that he died in Ethiopia, never having been to India.[23]

In addition to whatever importance may be attached to the possibility that Soliaman bin Haftoo was King Theodore's son, the account of his emigration from Ethiopia and his experiences in India provides firm documentation for the study of the migration and settlement of Ethiopians and other Africans in India. The testimonies of the petitioner, other troopers, and Major Prideaux are especially valuable in this connection.

The Community of African Descent
in Hyderabad City

It is clear that many Africans arrived in Hyderabad during the nineteenth century as slaves, servants, and freedmen, but the question

23. Richard Pankhurst to Joseph E. Harris, February 21, 1968. Pankhurst interviewed Meshesha's family and reported the results to me.

remains of how the community of African descent was established in the city. Its emergence was closely related to the history of the African Cavalry Guard. Like other components of the nizam's armed forces, the guard was quartered in a separate section of Hyderabad. The area in which the barracks for the African bodyguards and their families were located is still known as Siddi Risala ("African regiment"). It was a self-sufficient community in which the families of the guardsmen engaged in agriculture as their primary economic pursuit. Basketry, leather-working, and weaving were some of the other vocations of the inhabitants.[24]

As members of a separate community, the inhabitants of Siddi Risala were responsible for developing their own institutions and modes of life. Coming as they did from a variety of ethnic backgrounds and speaking different languages (some spoke Swahili, though few seem to speak it today), the Siddis found Islam to be their cultural common denominator. Most of the early guards had been recruited in Arabia and had become Muslim converts (Sunnites) prior to their arrival in Hyderabad. Thus, one of the first social institutions established in Siddi Risala was a mosque, with an accompanying Koranic school, which was attended by girls and those boys not in training to become members of the guard.

The community was under the direct control of the nizam who appointed his senior sergeant as village headman, or imam. He officiated at ceremonies and religious services and resolved minor problems in the community, such as fights, thefts, marital disputes, and so on.[25] Major cases and unpopular decisions were referred to the nizam's court. There seems to be no evidence of conflict, either religious or political, between Siddi Risala and the nizam. This was probably due to several factors: the appointed imam was the senior ranking African in the guard and a loyal servant of the nizam; the Siddis acknowledged their duty and allegiance to the nizam; the Sid-

24. Unless otherwise indicated, the remainder of this chapter is based on observations I made and oral testimonies I received in Hyderabad, January–February, 1968.

25. In January, 1968, Bilal bin Mabrook, former trooper in the guard, served in this capacity. He estimated his age to be about eighty; others said he was older.

dis, the nizam, and his other followers were all Sunnites; and the Siddis seem to have been reasonably well cared for as the king's private bodyguards.

A special problem the guardsmen faced was the lack of African women. All of the recruits were single men, and for a long time the only available African women were those few who were domestic servants, their daughters, and a few others who gravitated to the Siddi barracks. Gradually, those Siddis who did marry had daughters, but the number of women remained small, especially for Muslims who may have wanted more than one wife. The difficulty was somewhat resolved by the nizam, who encouraged and in some cases selected Arab girls to marry Siddis. While this helped solve the problem for some of the Siddis, it also added to the fears of the British that Arabs and Africans might unite to seize political control of Hyderabad.

The retention of African culture on the part of the Siddis was made difficult by the diversity of their linguistic and social backgrounds; the principal cultural aspect they shared was Islam, which was not indigenous to Africa. In addition, the fact that individual Africans were sometimes sold and resold several times in both Africa and Asia before arriving in India probably caused them to modify or add to their original culture. The Siddis did, however, retain certain aspects of their African culture — for example, musical instruments, folk songs, dances, and a few Swahili words interspersed in their Indian language, Urdu.

Following a performance during the India Republic Day celebrations in New Delhi in 1953, a troop of thirty-four Siddi folk dancers of Hyderabad received the following comments in an Indian daily:

> By far the most fascinating [dances] were the two most barbarous items: the Assamese Naga dances, unrivalled in their savage beauty and fantastic costume; and the equally savage and superbly rhythmic war dance of the African Bodyguards of the Nizam of Hyderabad — a piece of Africa transplanted in the 14th century into India, and never absorbed.[26]

Indians do acknowledge and, as the news report reveals, praise the Siddi dance; but they regard it as foreign and do not consider it to

26. *Statesman* (New Delhi), January 28, 1953.

be part of India's varied culture, in spite of the fact that the Siddis are citizens of the country.

The Siddis of Hyderabad are aware of their African ancestry. Nasir bin Muftah feels a close identity to Africa and considered emigrating there after India's independence; but, realizing that he was not in contact with anyone there, did not speak an African language, and was well established in India, he decided to stay in Hyderabad. However, most of the Hyderabadi Siddis are also sensitive about their traditional role as bonded guards and servants; they believe that their status resulted from their African background, their physical appearance, and stereotypes associated with them. While they regard themselves as Hyderabadis and Indians, they also recognize that they are different from others in the city and that they have been generally unaccepted as equals by other ethnic groups in India — including the Arabs, intermarriage with Arab women notwithstanding. But they are Muslims, identify themselves with the wider Muslim community (although the Hyderabadi Siddis still attend their own separate mosque), and are recognized (patronizingly, some Siddis think) as coreligionists by other Muslims, most of whom are of Arab descent.

The independence of India in 1947 highlighted the fact that Hyderabad was an overwhelmingly Hindu state under the rule of a Muslim, the nizam. He increasingly sought self-government and a closer union with Pakistan, which achieved independence in 1947 as a Muslim country. The nizam's refusal to accede to union on the terms offered by the Indian government led to the establishment of a blockade around Hyderabad. In September, 1948, troops of the Indian government overcame weak resistance and occupied the state. The nizam's rule was terminated, and thousands of Indian Muslims fled to Pakistan and to parts of Arabia. Some Hyderabadis estimate that at least 150,000 Muslims were "deported" at that time. Although it is impossible to know how many, if any, Siddis were part of that exodus, it is generally believed that most were not. In fact, the nizam retained his bodyguards until 1951, when he was finally forced to disband them. The Hyderabadi Siddis of today remain as symbols of the old Muslim order in which they, some Indians feel, received special privileges.

Life in Siddi Risala today is bleak. Few of its inhabitants are em-

113

ployed. Those who are perform menial tasks as domestics, cooks, porters, watchmen, or rickshaw drivers; a few are policemen. But employment opportunities in Hyderabad generally are very limited. The Siddis whose socioeconomic status is more elevated are the families of about 12 of the 500 khanazahs. The former nizam established a special trust fund for their maintenance. In 1968, for example, each family received 200 rupees (about $30) per month. Some of the Siddi khanazahs own small shops and restaurants and in general live much better than the average Indian.

There are other persons of African ancestry in the Hyderabad area. Many have no doubt been assimilated into the Arab-Indian population. But there are at least two localities on the outskirts of Hyderabad with names suggesting early African settlements. Siddipet ("African market"), located on the road between Hyderbad and Bidar, may represent a link in the history of African migration in that area. The inhabitants of the other area, Habshi Guda ("African village"), today claim Arab descent, but it is possible that intensive research there might reveal an earlier African community. It is possible that the ancestors of the current inhabitants are Africans whose origins can only be traced back to parts of Arabia. In any case, these communities deserve serious study because their names, their close historical relationship with Arabs and Africans, and the physical appearance of their inhabitants suggest an African origin.

There is no question about the African origin of Siddi Risala, now a community of about 2,000. But there is the possibility that the inhabitants will in time be assimilated by the Arabs and Indians because of the small number of "purely African women," which is estimated at about 200; one of the complaints of the Siddis is that the offspring of mixed Siddi-Arab marriages often "escape" into the wider community of Indians. Thus, the problem of reconstructing this aspect of Afro-Indian history is being complicated by intermarriage, the pressure of time, and the scarcity of available sources.

9.

Toward Assessing
the Afro-Asian Heritage

THE STORY of the African exodus to Asia is far from complete, partly because of the paucity of available records and partly because of the general lack of interest in this aspect of the diaspora. Nevertheless, some conclusions can be drawn. It is only partly true, for example, that African immigrants in Asia became absorbed into local societies. After centuries of existence in both Muslim and non-Muslim regions of Asia, Africans are still conspicuous because of their color and their status. Some Afro-Asian settlements are segregated, not by legal statutes but by a long history of stereotypes and myths which continue to have an unfavorable influence on both Asians and Afro-Asians. This raises the fundamental problem of the source of prejudice against the Africans in Asia. The question has been reserved for the last chapter because much of the answer awaits future research. However, in addition to the fact that organized ethnic groups or nationalities employ ethnocentricity to preserve their cultural and social order, there are more revealing clues to the genesis of black inferiority ideas in parts of Asia.

The Roots of Black Prejudice
in India and Iran

The inhabitants of the northern regions of India are for the most part Aryans (from whom the Brahmin caste claims descent) and therefore have a lighter complexion than southern Indians; it is generally accepted that the former have a color prejudice against the latter. Evidence of color prejudice in India may be traced back at least 5,000 years to the Rig-Veda, which is one of several ancient works forming the basis for Hindu religious beliefs. In several hymns of the Rig-Veda, Indra, the benevolent god and special champion of the Aryans, is referred to as driving away "the black skin, the dark-hued races, those darksome creatures, the noseless [flat-nosed] Das-yus." Although a fuller analysis is necessary to determine the extent to which the Rig-Veda was a source of color prejudice, even a cursory study reveals that value judgments were attached to color.[1] While some positive black symbols exist in Indian culture (some gods are black — Krishna, for example), much of Indian literature places a positive value on light skin. Many Indian languages use the words *fair* and *beautiful* synonymously. André Béteille cites the following Indian proverbs to illustrate value judgments made on color. From northern India: "A dark Brahmin, a fair Chuhra, a woman with a beard — these three are contrary to nature." "Do not cross a river with a black Brahmin or a fair Chamar." A southern Indian proverb advises: "Trust not a dark Brahmin or a fair Holeya."[2] Béteille observed, "In the popular image the Brahmin is regarded not only as fair, but also sharp-nosed, and as possessing, in general, more refined features," which "have a high social value" in India. He wrote, "a dark-skinned Brahmin girl is often a burden to the family because it is difficult to get a husband for her."[3] An examination in 1967 and 1968 of Indian newspaper advertisements for fair- or light-skinned brides confirmed Béteille's observation, though this kind of advertisement is becoming less popular. In any event, much more evidence must be obtained to explain the origin and extent of this sensitivity to blackness in India.

One factor that needs to be examined in great depth is the extent

1. Ralph T. H. Griffith, *Hymns of the Rigveda* (Benares, 1926), I, 130, 133, 181, 489, 611; and *ibid.*, II, 7, 296. See also the commentaries relating to each citation.

2. André Béteille, "Race and Descent as Social Categories in India," in *Color and Race*, ed. John Hope Franklin (Boston, 1968), pp. 174–76. Chuhra, Chamar, and Holeya are low castes; Brahmin, of course, is the highest caste.

3. André Béteille, *Caste, Class, and Power* (Berkeley, 1965), p. 48.

to which the centuries-old commercial and cultural contact between India and East Africa, which long predated the interaction of Europeans with either Indians or East Africans, contributed to the evolution of racial stereotypes, myths, and color prejudice. Much more should be known about the reception and subsequent status of those Africans who immigrated to India centuries before the period covered by this study. In what ways, if any, did the origin and development of the caste system apply to black people, either indigenous or African?[4] Moreover, endogamy has been an important means by which Indians have maintained their genetic identity, while Hindu law and custom have prevented significant intermixture with any outside group which would have modified the social and cultural identity and, consequently, the attitudes and behavior of Hindus. These are both fundamental issues related to the acceptance or rejection of Africans and Afro-Indians as equals.

Another important facet of this problem is the degree to which European — especially Portuguese and English — attitudes and actions had an impact on the Indians' value judgment of Africans. There is evidence that the concept of black inferiority had begun to develop in parts of Europe at least by the seventeenth century. Portugal had already commenced its slave trade in Africa, and other European countries — the Netherlands, France, and England in particular — were soon to follow suit. Racial attitudes were decisive factors in the social relationships between Europeans and Africans in Africa, the Americas, and elsewhere. It is therefore highly probable that when Europeans extended the slave trade into India, their derogatory attitude toward Africans affected the attitudes of Indians. Such a result is all the more likely because the era of the slave trade by Westerners was accompanied by European rationalizations of their activities in Africa. It was a time when European scholars, scientists, and writers generally popularized theories of black inferiority, which became part of "scientific knowledge." The dissemination of such propaganda convinced many people throughout the world that black

4. Several Western writers have linked the caste system in India to race and color, as have a number of Indian writers — C. Roy, N. K. Dutt, and G. S. Ghurye. Their views are discussed by a leading Indian authority, D. N. Majumdar, in *Races and Cultures in India* (Bombay, 1958), p. 307.

people were inferior and therefore were not worthy of treatment as equals. The question, however, remains: To what extent did those European myths affect the racial beliefs of Indians.

Racialism in Iran can be explained by the same line of reasoning which applies to India. Like their Aryan neighbors in northern India, Iranians are generally color-conscious. A fair or light complexion is regarded as the ideal color for human beauty. A preliminary investigation suggested that Iranian tradition also attaches a stigma to blackness. Several informants in Tehran, Isfahan, Shiraz, and Bandar Abbas related similar proverbial expressions. When a person is being neglected by relatives or friends he may ask, for example, "Am I your child of a Negress?" An expression for irresponsibility and lack of sound judgment is "It is like putting a sword in the hands of a drunken Negro." While these sayings are few in number and are by no means intended to characterize Iran or Iranians in general, they were repeated in virtually the same way several times in widely separated parts of the country. This is certainly not enough evidence to explain adequately the kind of scorn which, some members of the black community near Bandar Abbas feel, is directed at them and which, some Iranians agree, exists.[5] Nor does this necessarily explain the isolation of the community of African descent near Jiruft, mentioned in Chapter 6. The sources of Iranian views and treatment of Africans are embedded deeply in Persian culture and history. For example, the ancient contacts with Africans during the early centuries of legitimate trade as well as the slave trade, which took many Africans to the Persian Gulf region, have affected Iranian attitudes toward blacks.

The slave trade and slavery were decisive in Africa's relations with the outside world. The slave trade to Asia continued for more than a thousand years and left untold numbers, very likely millions, of Africans scattered throughout the continent. Since the institution of slavery, resulting from economic motives, was supported by stereotypes and prejudice, one may conclude that the Asian exploitation

5. This information is based on oral accounts recorded by the author in Iran (Tehran, Shiraz, and Bandar Abbas) in 1967. Those interviewed were Iranian students, professors, businessmen, and civil servants; American Peace Corps Volunteers; and British teachers.

of Africans, as in the Western world, necessarily warped men's minds and institutions for centuries. Asians, like Europeans, were primarily interested in exploiting African labor; therefore, they nourished ideas in support of social and political systems that protected and perpetuated those interests. In Asia, Africans provided the labor for the date plantations and the pearl-diving industry; they were the principal stevedores, crew hands, and domestics, the troops of Asian rulers, and the eunuchs and concubines of Asian elites. All of these roles satisfied the psychological, social, and economic needs of the Asian slaveholder and contributed to the devaluation of the worth of Africans. It is significant that for the most part Afro-Asians still occupy these same roles, if they have employment at all.

Cultural Survival
in India

It is important to note that the voyage from Africa to Asia did not obliterate the slave's memory of his homeland. This is attested to by statements from many slaves who were liberated by the British during the nineteenth century. The statements were made to a British official — a police commissioner, ship captain, or consul — in the presence of a third person as witness. All statements were made orally and recorded by the official or his deputy. One girl, Zainab, testified to the police commissioner of Bombay that she had been captured in Ethiopia, taken to Jedda and, after about two years, to Bombay. She said her real name was Imani, the name Zainab having been given to her by her first master. Another girl slave, Nur, testified that she had been sold at her home in Gurage (Ethiopia) and within about a year was taken to Bombay via Jedda. Jamilah, also a female slave, recalled her village in Ethiopia. She gave her father's name as Dissa and her own as Aiyant. She had arrived in Bombay via Jedda.[6] A liberated African male recalled being captured in his village near Dar es Salaam. Another remembered being seized while playing with

6. These statements were taken by the Bombay commissioner of police, March 23, 1882 (see Appendix 1).

119

other children in Malindi. Fomi Merima testified that his village was Mohogoni, near Dar es Salaam. His original name was Moshenzi. Abdulla Nekanbi said he was from Bagamoyo. He had been captured and shipped to the Batinah coast, where he worked for a while on a date farm. Maybrook Miao recalled having been shipped as a slave from Kilwa. The fugitive slave Hadaya explained that she had been brought with 130 other slaves from Kilwa and unloaded at Ras Rasheim. Four other slaves — Marjan, Farzullah, Ubidi, and Mabrok — testified that they were from Zanzibar where they had been captured ten years earlier.[7]

The problem of cultural survival is a complicated one. Only with the greatest difficulty could even the symbols of an African culture survive the destructiveness of slavery. Slaves were captured during raids and were marched in chains to the coast. They were indiscriminately separated from friends and relatives when they were sold within Africa and in Asia. This harsh experience, together with life as a bonded person in a dominant, alien, and generally hostile society, gradually caused the African to forget most of his native language and to modify his traditional way of life, his religious beliefs, and indeed his psyche. But that experience, as decisive as it was in many ways, did not destroy his consciousness of the African heritage. His heritage was what bound him to slavery and denigration, even after manumission. His physical features identified him as an African, set him apart, and usually assured him only a menial status. His strangeness reinforced his awareness of his African background and in some cases caused him to wish he could escape it. Neither the Asians (Muslim and Hindu) nor the Europeans allowed the Africans to emerge to full group equality. Derogatory comments, such as those about Malik Ambar in the seventeenth century, continued into the twentieth century, as evidenced by the descriptions in 1953 of the "barbarous"

7. These statements were taken by S. B. Miles, consul judge at Muscat, December 8, 1884, and by the Bombay commissioner of police, September 2, 1887. See also India, External Department, October, 1887, sec. A, p. 282; and Appendix 1. In both Iran and India there are persons of African descent who can recall their relatives' and friends' accounts of their original homes. Personal interviews are the best way to collect this information. One must be careful not to be misled by claims of an Arab background, which, as indicated in Chapter 8, is not always correct.

Siddi dancers in India. Nonetheless, as noted in Chapter 8, the Siddi community in Hyderabad has retained its traditional African musical instruments and dances, a few Swahili words, and memories of Africa, however blurred by time. A more intensive study of this community very likely would reveal other indications of cultural survival.

C. F. Beckingham and Richard Pankhurst detect a possible cultural relationship between Ethiopia and the former Muslim kingdom of Khandesh, just north of Ahmadnagar. It seems that Habshis in Khandesh may have imprisoned the male members of their ruling dynasty on the closely guarded mountain of Asirgarh in much the same way as some Ethiopians imprisoned their royalty on the Ambar Geshen mountain in Ethiopia.[8]

Islam as an Agent
of Assimilation

Since the Muslim Arabs were the principal traders and owners of African slaves in Asia, the role of Islam in the reception and adjustment of Africans in Asian society deserves some analysis. First of all, Islam did not regard slaves as chattels but as people with souls who were accepted as such in the faith. In addition, the Koran called for humane treatment of slaves; the manumission of a slave was regarded as a meritorious act. Many Africans converted to Islam in Africa and Asia and were accepted as clergymen, military commanders, political advisers, and sometimes kings. Thus, Islam's egalitarianism seemed confirmed, thereby enhancing its appeal to Africans.

Another appeal of Islam is that it does not require converts to abandon traditional beliefs which can be adjusted or tolerated by the faith. For example, Muslim theology tolerates practices of divination, magic, witchcraft, and sorcery when they are applied toward such legitimate aims as curing disease, preventing or ameliorating misfortune, assuring success, or apprehending criminals. The rationale

8. C. F. Beckingham, "Ambar Geshen and Asirgarh," *Journal of Semitic Studies* (1957) ; and Richard Pankhurst, *An Introduction to the Economic History of Ethiopia* (London, 1961), p. 422.

for this is that the achievement of such aims depends on the will of Allah. Over many centuries these and other African practices were absorbed by Islam.

The assimilative character of Islam is further attested to by the way in which traditional embodiments of supreme power have been identified with Allah. The Cushite god *waq* (among the Galla and Somali in Ethiopia, Somali, and Sudan) and the Swahili god *mangu* have both a traditional and an Islamic significance.[9] Islam has also accommodated the traditional reverence for ancestors by accepting them as intermediaries between man and the Prophet. Thus prayers are rendered for and through but not to the ancestors. A specific example comes from East Africa: Somali Islam venerates not only the great Muslim founders of the tariqas (brotherhoods) but also local saints, for their piety and work, and local founders of lineage groups.[10]

Africans, therefore, could easily identify with Islam, which provided them with an enduring heritage, reinforced a kind of brotherhood among them, and built bridges, however imperfect, to the surrounding community. As was pointed out earlier, Africans had a long experience as members and proselytizers of Islam, and many of them came to Persia and India as Muslims, having converted in either Africa or Arabia. The faith had accepted various aspects of African culture and reinforced certain practices, such as polygyny. Arabic was for many Africans a vehicular language which transcended other Asian as well as indigenous African languages. Many Africans and Afro-Asians also recall that Bilal was the African slave whose stentorian voice made him the first muezzin (caller for prayer services) of Islam. His freedom was purchased, and he became a close adviser of the Prophet Mohammed. To be sure, many Africans came to regard Islam as "a black man's religion." Furthermore, where sizable communities of Muslim Africans settled in Asia, they generally constructed their own mosque, which served as a community center, a

9. I. M. Lewis, "The Names of God in Northern Somali," *Bulletin of the School of Oriental and African Studies*, XXII, 134–40; J. S. Trimingham, *Islam in East Africa* (Oxford, 1964), p. 78; and I. M. Lewis, *Islam in Tropical Africa* (Oxford, 1966), p. 261.

10. Lewis, *Islam in Tropical Africa*, p. 61.

school, and a place of worship. In these ways Islam facilitated a cohesiveness within the Afro-Asian communities.

African Assertion
of Power

Since Afro-Asians were conscious of their African heritage and were generally alienated, largely because of that heritage, and since the bond that united them was Islam, it is understandable that the principal thrusts for power were made by Islamized Africans in parts of Persia, Bengal, the Deccan, and Janjira. Those areas had concentrations of Africans who established unity among themselves and links with others, mostly Arabs. When an African did usurp political power, in each case he had the support of fellow Africans who formed the core of the coup. Once in power the African leadership appointed Africans to key positions in the administration and organized and maintained an African guard.

Malik Ambar probably regarded himself as the originator of an African dynasty in the Deccan. But although he successfully controlled and made important contributions to the political, economic, and cultural developments of the Deccan, he was unable to assure the continuity of African power through the establishment of a practical system of succession which would have guaranteed rule by his son. Ambar did, however, establish diplomatic and military links with the other African power in the region, the Siddis of Janjira, whom he appointed as his naval squadron. It seems noteworthy that he did not conclude such an agreement with the coastal Marathas, with and for whom he fought on several occasions. But the Siddis had the stronger navy. It seems reasonable to conclude that the Siddis' identity, as well as their power, caused Malik Ambar to choose them as an ally.

The Bengali Africans (see pp. 79–80), Malik Ambar, and the Siddis of Janjira are examples of Africans who searched for and acquired political power in India; but the Siddis of Bombay and Hyderabad apparently made no such attempt. In the case of Bombay, most Siddis were descendants of liberated Africans who had been distributed among various Indian families whose background and status, the English hoped, would encourage the Africans to become Christians. Other liberated and runaway Africans migrated to Bombay to secure employment. Neither of these groups established a strong African community but were instead dispersed throughout the city. Indeed, freed Africans living with Indian families identified themselves with the larger community, not because they were readily accepted by that community but largely because they hoped to survive as equals in Indian society, in the absence of an African settlement which could fulfill their economic and spiritual demands. Thus, over the years the identity of many Siddis became blurred by intermarriage and by the dwindling of their numbers.

The case of the Hyderabadi Siddis is somewhat different. Africans have long inhabited that city, and for over a hundred years there has been a small but compact community of Africans there. Even today, although there has not been any significant immigration into Siddi Risala for more than fifty years, the estimated population is 2,000. That settlement, as has been pointed out, is generally aware of its African background, physically and culturally, and has maintained some African cultural forms. It has its own mosque, and the community is supervised by a Siddi. For years the Siddis have remained poor and alienated from the larger community. Yet, they apparently have made no effort to gain political power for themselves, though at one time the British feared that a coalition between the Siddis and Arabs would have that result. The fact that this did not occur, in spite of the several ties between the Siddis and Arabs, further reveals the extent of African alienation from other groups of Hyderabad.

Several reasons may be given for the passivity of the Hyderabadi Siddis. They were a heterogeneous group without a common indigenous language or culture; until 1951 (when the nizam disbanded his bodyguards) the Africans were always a small minority, although privileged in the sense of having social and economic status as the nizam's guards; they were Muslims who identified with the nizam and his court; they were never fully armed as a group, serving principally as valets, cooks, and servants, with only a few as real bodyguards; and finally, as a small, generally unaccepted group, their main security and support depended on their loyalty to the nizam.

Even within the Siddi group there was competition for advancement in rank and privilege — note, for example, the position of the khana-zahs. Furthermore, the Siddi who went to school received a Koranic education, which did not inform him of the forces controlling his position or point out ways in which he might improve his lot. Indeed, Siddi Risala has remained a parochial community with a fatalistic acceptance of the status quo.

Clearly, therefore, Islam has in some cases served as a pacifier, a means of facilitating accommodation to the customs and controls of the dominant group; in other cases, it has provided some upward mobility, which sometimes encouraged violent thrusts for greater political power.

Why Not Pan-Africanism?

Afro-Asians do not seem to have been influenced at all by Pan-Africanism in the context of either Asia or the world.[11] Malik Ambar's alliance with the Siddis of Janjira does not appear to have been based on any ideology of black or African solidarity, but was more likely an effort to strengthen his position against the Mughuls. Although the identity factor was probably important, it was not primary.

During the twentieth century, African and Afro-American appeals for Pan-African unity do not seem to have been directed to Afro-Asians. Of the Asians who presented general petitions to the peace conference of 1918 in Paris, where the second Pan-African conference was also convening, none was of African descent; neither they nor delegates to the Pan-African conference expressed any concern about Afro-Asians. This observation is typical of the history of the Pan-African movement, whose leaders have seemed unaware of the African presence in Asia. Perhaps the primary reason for this is that the search for international solidarity among blacks was, until 1945, essentially a movement founded and directed by blacks in

11. I found no Afro-Asian who had ever heard of Marcus Garvey, W. E. B. DuBois, Kwame Nkrumah, or Duse Mohamed. The last-named operated out of Egypt and published the *African Times and Orient Review* from 1912 to 1920. See Duse Mohamed, *In the Land of the Pharaohs* (London, 1968).

the United States and the West Indies; the movement emerged from the experience of racism, which not only physically enslaved Africans but also distorted much of their history and culture. Because racism in the United States and the West Indies was far more intense than that in Asia, many black Americans came to believe that their physical and cultural salvation depended on their identification with Africa and their personal involvement in the elevation of all persons of African descent. That black Americans were generally unaware of the Afro-Asians is explained simply by geographical distance; by slavery and segregation, which restricted physical and intellectual mobility; and by Western education, which did not concern itself in any important way with Africans or their descendants. In 1945 control of the Pan-African movement shifted to the African leadership. Even then, however, the principal leaders were West Africans who were not aware of the Afro-Asians for the same reasons as the Afro-Americans; furthermore, they were occupied with the immediate political demands of their own countries and of Africa in general. The principal East African leader, Jomo Kenyatta, was deeply involved with solidifying a political base in Kenya and maintaining links with West African leaders.

In the final analysis, however, Afro-Asians did not organize and assert themselves forcefully enough to attract the attention of Africans or blacks elsewhere. They were scattered over wide areas in Asia, frequently unknown even by their immediate neighbors. As slaves, assimilated into Islam and not concentrated in large communities, they were unable to develop a meaningful black or African consciousness out of which a "back to Africa" movement or a locally based, black nationalist tradition could emerge. Although some Africans did return to Africa (the Bombay Africans, for example), their return was not intended to establish a strong base of African power; it was supervised by Europeans who, in addition to whatever humanitarian motives they may have had, were also concerned with protecting their East African interests, as missionaries, merchants, or colonial officials. In short, the Bombay Africans and others like them made a significant impact on East African history; but their return to Africa and their activities there were unrelated to the problems of Afro-Asians.

There seems to be no record in Asian history of Afro-Asians seeking political power outside the context of Asia. The history of revolts and other pressures have all been attempts to reconcile the Africans' differences with other Asians within the existing political structures. Malik Ambar and the Siddis of Janjira and Bengal sought the cooperation of other Asians with whom they identified in common political struggles. Available evidence supports the conclusion that the historical inequities suffered by Africans in Asia have not created the push, nor have the contemporary affirmations of Africans and Afro-Americans generated the pull, necessary for any political identification of Asian blacks with Africa or the international black power movements in the United States and the West Indies.

The heritage of Islam, the absence of obtrusive racism, the intermarriage between Africans and Arabs, the decreasing numbers of Africans in Afro-Asian communities, the integrative policies of Asian nations, and the lack of effective exposure to developments of blacks in other parts of the world all account for the fact that Asians of African descent have increasingly accommodated themselves to the slow and agonizing process of racial and cultural oblivion.

APPENDIX 1

SLAVE STATEMENTS*

During the nineteenth century a number of slaves appealed to the British authorities for their freedom on the grounds that they had been abused by their masters or that they had been brought into the country illegally. The following statements, obviously edited by the recorders, represent their testimonies.

Statement of Salim (March, 1837)

I am a slave; I was brought from Sanar [Sennar] to Suarkin [Suakin], and from thence to Mocha and there sold to Hoor sie Yoseph,

* This material was taken from: Bombay, External Department, May, 1855, sec. A, pp. 131–41; India, Political Department, July, 1883, sec. A, I, 14–25; *idem*, External Department, October, 1887, sec. A, pp. 278–93; *ibid.*, November, 1887, sec. A, pp. 9–10; *Irish University Press Series of British Parliamentary Papers* (Shannon, 1969), *Slave Trade*, LXXXVIII, 178–79. The statements of Salim and Suigar were recorded by the British consul in Muscat; Hadaya's statement was recorded by a captain on board the British cruiser *Osprey*; the others were recorded by the Bombay commissioner of police. The statements are presented in full as they appear in the documents; in some cases, I have been able to identify place names.

who sent me on board the Futteh Kurreem, to be sold at this or any other place. I do not come with my own consent.

Statement of Suigar (March, 1837)

I am a slave; my master the nacoda bought me at Mutra. I was taken to Jave, Achen [Aden] and Penang, but never allowed to quit the ship. I receive no wages. I did not come of my own consent. I was told to go with my master. I was originally from another country. People came and spread dates and fat; I was hungry, and took some to eat. Then they carried me away. I have neither father nor mother. I was sold for five dollars.

Statement of Zafran (March, 1882)

I am a native of a village in Abyssinia. I do not know the names of my parents, nor am I aware whether they are alive or dead. When young I was caught at my native village by an African, who took me to a distant place, where I was sold by him to another African. After having passed through several hands, I was eventually sold to Hafiz Abdul Kaiyum at Mecca. I do not know the name of the several persons through whose hands I have passed. I am not willing to go with Hafiz Abdul Kaiyum. I pray that I may be liberated and sent back to Jeddah where I am desirous of residing. My former name was Bilela, and the name of Zafran was given me by one of my purchasers.

Statement of Zainab (March, 1882)

I am a native of Seka in Abyssinia. About two years ago an African stole me from my native village and sold me at Gojam to an Arab named Haji Ahmed who took me to Jeddah, where I was purchased by a Memon, called Haji Kasim. A month ago Hafiz Abdul Kaiyum and his brother bought me of[f] Haji Kasim and brought me together with two other girls to Bombay. I am not willing to go with Hafiz Abdul Kaiyum. I pray that Government will kindly do what they may consider best for me. My former name was Imani, and the name of Zainab has been given me by Memon Haji Kasim.

Statement of Nur (March, 1882)

I am a native of Guragay [Gurage] in Abyssinia. About a year

ago my parents sold me to an Arab Christian from whom I was purchased by an Arab, who took me to Jeddah. At Jeddah, after having
passed through the hands of three or four dealers in slaves, I was
bought by Memon Haji Kasim, who sold me to Hafiz Abdul Kaiyum.
I do not wish to go with Hafiz Abdul Kaiyum. My former name was
Turungo. I have been called Nur since my purchase by Hafiz Abdul
Kaiyum.

Statement of Jamilah (March, 1882)

I am a native of a village called Wachala in Abyssinia. My father's
name is Dissa. I do not know my mother's name. I am not aware
whether my parents are now dead or alive. A few years ago an African named Badassa caught me at my native village when my parents
were absent, and took me to another village, the name of which I do
not know. At that place Badassa sold me to one Ahmed who, after
having taken me to several places, eventually carried me to Jeddah
where I was sold by him to an Arab named Hasan. I was afterwards
taken to Mecca and purchased there by Arab Hussein, who after some
time sold me to Hafiz Abdul Kaiyum. Suliaman and Hussein are
dealers in slaves. I do not wish to go with Hafiz Abdul Kaiyum. I
request that Government will kindly do what they consider best for
me. I pray that I may no longer be kept as a slave to any person. I
was purchased by Hafiz Abdul Kaiyum about eight months ago. My
former name was Aiyant. I have been called Jamilah since I was purchased by Hafiz Abdul Kaiyum.

Statement of Sultan Merima (1884)

I am a free man and lived at Kanduchi, near Dar es Salaam. I was
seized one night by the Arabs and put in a dhow with 120 others and
brought to the Batinah by an Arab named Marimo. I was two months
in Batinah and was then taken in a small boat with six other slaves
to Shemal.

Statement of Mabrook Nyassa (1884)

I am a slave of one Khamees bin Muhammad, an Arab of Soweyk.
I am originally from Malindi, where I was a free man. I used to cultivate the ground. I was playing at Malindi with some children on the

131

beach where the Arabs seized me. I never seized and sold any children myself. There were 70 slaves in the bughla that brought me over.
We landed at Soweyk in the Batinah. I was three months at Soweyk
and was taken to the pirate coast where I was sold. This was ten days
before the man-of-war came and took me.

Statement of Fomi Merima (1884)

I am a native of Mohogoni, near Dar es Salaam, and I am a free
man [named] Moshenzi. I am a cultivator. I was seized by a man of
Dar es Salaam named Dosi and sold to the Arabs. I never sold children to Arabs. I was shipped at Kanduchi in a large vessel with many
slaves, perhaps 200. Many of them died on the way. When near Soor
[Sur] we saw a white steamer with three masts, and the Arabs were
afraid and put us down below, but the ship passed out of sight, and
we were then allowed to come up. We were landed first at Soor and
then taken to the Batinah, from whence we were taken to the Shemal
and sold. I had been there twelve days when the man-of-war arrived
and rescued us.

Statement of Khamees Merima (1884)

I belong to Kanduchi and am a free man. I was seized one day by
an Arab named Saeed and shipped at Windi in a bughla with 44
slaves. We were landed at Shargah. The dhow did not stop at Soor
or at the Batinah. This was about five months ago when the dates
were small and unripe.

Statement of Abdulla Nekanbi of Bagamoyo (1884)

One Mahamesi seized me one day and sold me to the Arabs. I was
shipped at Windi. The dhow had 64 men and 50 women, and we were
landed at Batinah. I remained in the Batinah from the time the dates
were small, four or five months ago, to the Bakri-eed two months ago,
when I was taken to the Shemal for sale. I had been there six weeks
when the man-of-war arrived. I was imported in the same dhow as
the last man, Khamees.

Statement of Maybrook Miao (1884)

I was shipped at Kilwa in a dhow with many slaves by an Arab named Ali. We were landed at Soweyk, where I remained three months, and was then taken on to the Shemal by sea. I had been there one month when the man-of-war rescued us. We had been brought down in chain gangs from the Yao country to this coast.

Statement of Hadaya, a fugitive slave (1887)

I was brought here three years ago from Kilwa in a dhow with 130 other slaves. We were landed at Ras Rasheim. I was sold to an Arab named Hamad bin Khamis for 30 dollars. He lives at Kaddeh, about ten miles from Ras Madraka. I lived with him till he died last year. I am married to Mabrook, a slave of my late master, by whom I have no children. I left my husband because he is always at sea and I am left by myself. In the morning I am sent to drive goats till the evening, when I return and have some work to do and cook the food. In the morning I have to drive the goats again and I do not get enough food to eat [or any] clothes. I get grumbled at and get beaten by my Arab master. If I am returned to my master he will sell me to another tribe where I shall get hard treatment. Last year I ran away. [When I returned] my master tied me up with a rope three days and beat me. My husband is employed in a fishing boat and is away employed fishing, and I am left with the Arab, my master, who treats me badly.

Statements of Farzullah, Marjan, Ubidi, and Mabrok (August, 1888)

They said they are natives of Kirwa in Zanzibar; that about ten years ago they were taken to Zanzibar [city] by a Suri and sold as slaves to another Arab, who then sold them to one Muhammad bin Ali at Punna [Poona]; that they remained in his services up to within a month ago, when in consequence of repeated ill treatment they absconded, and taking some provisions, seized a small sailing boat and put to sea; that after being driven about by the wind in various directions, they came in sight of a ship and on being seen were taken aboard by the Captain and brought to Bombay; that they are willing to work for a living in whatever way the Government may order.

133

APPENDIX 2

LIST OF AFRICAN SLAVES CAPTURED
IN CUTCH, 1841*

1. In the boat Ram Pussa; tindal and owner, Nakwo Jaffer Budhal:
Man named Nusseeba, about 40 years old, purchased for 20 dollars at Muscat by Beereeata Hussain, for the alleged purpose of being used in his boat and in his house.

2. In the Sejal Pussa; tindal, Malim Nursee; owner, Tukur Waljei Hunsavee:
Boy named Bhoorakoo, about 12 years old, purchased at Zanzibar, by Sekh Gool Mahomed, at the price of 20½ dollars, for his household service.
Boy named Kamees, about 12 years old, purchased at Zanzibar for 19 dollars, by Tukur Magjee Monauvee, to be employed in his garden.
Man named Moeerjeh Mehgee, about 22 years old, bought at Zanzibar for 25 dollars, by Tukur Heeja Oomursee, to be employed on his land in the village of Bhamnajee.

* This material was taken from *Irish University Press Series of British Parliamentary Papers* (Shanon, 1969), *Slave Trade*, LXXXVIII, 229–30.

3. In the Kadureeya; tindal and owner, Nakwo Dado; the boat is mortgaged to Sah Veekumsee Tejpall:

Boy, named Mohbo, about 11 years old, bought by the tindal at Mombasur [Mombasa], for 20 dollars, to be employed in the boat.

Boy, named Nusseeba, about 15 years old, bought for 20 dollars, and brought over by Abrahim, in place of another slave whom he left to take care of his property at Mombasur.

Man, named Kamees, about 25 years of age. This slave is sent by Luckoo, of Mombasur, in charge of Tukur Kutoo Dhunjee, for delivery to Treeko at Mandavie, who has absconded some time ago.

4. In the Gunjoo Sularuntee; tindal, Nakwo Abdulla Syanee; owner, Tukur Peetha Mohunjee:

Boy, named Jummo, about 14 years old, bought at Zanzibar for 19 dollars, by the tindal, to be employed in the boat.

Boy, named Villeydhee, about 10 years old, commissioned by Tukur Pisso, and purchased at Zanzibar for 20 dollars, to be employed as a playfellow with the tukur's children.

5. In the Koteeah Vusseesul; tindal, Savee; owner, Gopall Juthanee:

Boy, named Singorah, about 10 years old, purchased at Zanzibar for 18 dollars, by the tindal, for the purpose of being adopted as his heir, he being himself childless.

6. In the Gunjah; tindal, Pabho Pudumsee Malim; owner, Premjei Jethanee:

Man, named Singorah, about 22 years old, exchanged by the tindal, at Zanzibar, for another slave who had been long in his hand.

Boy, named Nusseeba, about 10 years old, commissioned by Waeevet Bhayeco Salanee, for his own use, in the service of his boat and family, and purchased at Zanzibar for 13 dollars.

7. In the Tutchkheir; tindal, Kheto Malim; owner, Tukur Morarjei Bhanjee; chartered by Tukur Gopall Mowjee:
Man, named Bhuracks, about 20 years old, bought for 20 dollars at Mombasur by the tindal, to be employed in his boat.

In the Runchor Pussa; tindal, Abhoo Malim, owner, Gopall Mowjee:

A man named Bhuraks, about 25 years old; a woman named Tumusa, about 13 years old; a man named Saleem, about 18 years old; a woman named Byahtee, about 15 years old; a man named Vilbhidhee, about 18 years old; a woman named Kumeesah, about 16 years old; a man named Hussein, about 16 years old; a woman named Byahtee, about 13 years old.

The four women were married to the four men, and the whole batch belongs to Tukur Jetha Maljei, who has been for some time a resident at Zanzibar, and has made use of these slaves in carrying on his business there; the tukur has brought them with him to Mandavie, because there is no one at Zanzibar in whose charge he could leave them; he has shut up his shop there during his visit to Cutch, but intends to carry the slaves back with him, when he returns to resume his business next season.

[There were two other women]: Meydoree, aged about 15; and Mygiddo, aged about 12. These two girls belong to the establishment of Tukur Copall Mowjee, at Zanzibar, and are sent over to be married to two of the slaves in the tukur's house at Mandavie.

8. In the Buggalow Sullamutee; tindal, Nakwo Hussein; owner, Gopall Mowjee:

A man, named Mukhboo, about 20 years old, sent by Tukur Soorjei, of Mombasur, to Treeko Mohundavee, to be taken care of, the man having been picked up destitute and unowned.

9. In the Buttalah Luckonee Tussa; tindal, Ramjee; owner, Mahadeo Thofun:

A boy, named Asmanee, about 15 years old.

A girl, named Husseemah, about 12 years old.

These form part of the household of Jairam Seujee, at Zanzibar, and were sent by him, the boy as carpenter to the vessel, the girl for the service of his family, who reside at Moondra.

> (A true translation)
> (signed) P. M. Melvill
> First Assistant Resident
> (A true translation)
> (signed) Henry Pottinger
> Resident in Cutch

BIBLIOGRAPHICAL ESSAY

THE PRINCIPAL REASON for this book is that to date there has been no general account of African migration to and settlement in Asia. Since any study of this nature must first examine aspects of the East African slave trade, some comments about the literature on this subject are appropriate.

The East African Slave Trade

No single book, or even group of books, does justice to this important historical event; but there are a few studies which, when supplemented with data from primary sources, provide a satisfactory background for an examination of the African slave trade to Asia. *The East African Slave Trade* by Edward A. Alpers, published in 1967 for the Historical Association of Tanzania, is the best available account; it is up to date and approaches the subject from the perspective of Africa and the African. But it is essentially a pamphlet (26 pp.) and raises more questions than can be answered at this stage of research. The two standard works by Reginald Coupland, *East Africa and Its Invaders* (Oxford, 1938) and *The Exploitation of East Africa 1856–1890: The Slave Trade and the Scramble* (1939; reprint ed., Evanston, Ill., 1967), focus on various aspects of East African history; but there are some useful sections on the slave trade, especially in the former book. Although there is no specific chapter

on the subject, very helpful discussions of the slave trade are interspersed throughout Roland Oliver and Gervase Mathew, *History of
East Africa* (London, 1963), Vol. I; and B. A. Ogot and J. A. Kieran,
Zamani: A Survey of East African History (New York, 1968). James
Duffy, *A Question of Slavery* (Cambridge, Mass., 1967) gives a very
creditable account of late-nineteenth- and early-twentieth-century slav-
ery in the Portuguese colonies of Angola and Mozambique. J. B. Kelly,
Britain and the Persian Gulf, 1795–1880 (Oxford, 1968) presents
an excellent account of British diplomacy and the slave trade in the
Persian Gulf as well as in India.

Various aspects of the slave trade are illuminated by the following
works, especially those written by first-hand observers: Lieutenant
Barnard, *Three Years' Cruise in the Mozambique Channel for the
Suppression of the Slave Trade* (London, 1848); E. F. Berlioux, *The
Slave Trade in Africa in 1872* (London, 1872); P. Colomb, *Slave
Catching in the Indian Ocean* (London, 1873); Reginald Coupland,
The Anti-Slavery Movement (London, 1933); H. Darley and N. A.
Sharp, *Slave Trading and Slave Owning in Abyssinia* (London, 1922);
Pierre V. A. Ferret and Joseph G. Galinier, *Voyage en Abyssinie*
(Paris, 1847–48); Richard Gray, *A History of the Southern Sudan
1839–1889* (Oxford, 1961); G. B. Hill, *Colonel Gordon in Central
Africa* (London, 1887); Pascoe G. Hill, *Fifty Days on Board a Slave
Vessel* (London, 1873); Edward Hutchinson, *The Slave Trade of
East Africa* (London, 1874); Bombay, Miscellaneous Information
Connected with the Persian Gulf, n.s., no. 24 (1856), "Paper Relative
to the Measures Adopted by the British Government, between the
Years 1820 and 1844, for Effecting the Suppression of the Slave
Trade in the Persian Gulf," prepared by Lt. A. B. Kemball; David
Livingstone, *Narrative of an Expedition to the Zambesi and Its Tribu-
taries, and the Discovery of the Lakes Shirwa and Nyassa* (London,
1865); E. A. Loftus, *Elton and the East African Coast Slave Trade*
(London, 1952); Richard Pankhurst, *An Introduction to the Economic History of Ethiopia* (London, 1961), and "The Ethiopian
Slave Trade in the Nineteenth and Early Twentieth Centuries: A Statistical Inquiry," *Journal of Semitic Studies*, Vol. IX, no. 1 (Spring,
1964); Romolo Gessi Pasha, *Seven Years in the Sudan* (London,
1892); Charles E. B. Russell, *General Rigby, Zanzibar and the Slave*

Trade (London, 1935); Henry Salt, *A Voyage to Abyssinia* (London, 1814); E. Blondeel van Cuelebroeck, *Rapport général de Blondeel sur son expèdition en Abyssinie* (Brussels, 1839–42); C. S. Nicholls, *The Swahili Coast* (London, 1971).

There are of course many other travel accounts that mention the slave trade, but I have included only those which have contributed the most to this particular study. Even in some of these, however, the references are scattered throughout and sometimes add little to what is already known.

Africans in Indian History

Primary Sources. The government of Bombay, which reported to the Court of Directors of the East India Company, supervised British relations with the Persian Gulf area until 1873, when the government of India assumed that responsibility. While most records of those relations pertain to the Persian Gulf region, a considerable amount of information deals with East Africa. The Bombay government supervised relations through its Political and Secret departments, while the government of India did the same through its Political, Home, and External departments. The bulk of the records kept by those departments is located in the National Archives of India, in New Delhi; daily records of East India Company officials are found in the *Public Department Diaries* and the *Surat Factory Diaries*, both available in the Secretariat Record Office, Elphinstone College Building, in Bombay.

There are a few catalogues available as guides to the use of the materials referred to above: V. G. Dighe, *Descriptive Catalogue of the Secret and Political Department Series, 1755–1820* (Bombay, 1954); George W. Forrest, *Alphabetical Catalogue of the Contents of the Bombay Secretariat Records, 1630–1780* (Bombay, 1887); India, *A Handbook to the Records of the Government of India in the Imperial Record Department, 1748–1859* (Calcutta, 1925); R. Hughes Thomas, *Selections from the Records of the Bombay Government: Historical and Other Information Connected with the Province of Oman, Muskat, Bahrein, and Other Places in the Persian Gulf* (Bombay, 1856), n.s. no. 24. These are very useful catalogues, but they have missed many references to Africans in India. This seems to have resulted from their strict reliance on the subject headings in the margins of the daily entries in the diaries. Those headings, of course, reflect the primary interest of the recorder; but in several instances the African slave trade, African slaves, and free Africans were discussed by some of the East India Company agents in their general reports on customs, finance, supplies, the military, and various inspections. Since the presence of Africans in India has not been an important concern of either Europeans or Indians, and since so little research has been conducted on the subject, the researcher is advised to use such catalogues as guides only and to investigate thoroughly the documents themselves.

Several of the state archives contain valuable materials. In addition to those in New Delhi and Bombay, the State Archives of Andhra Pradesh in Hyderabad contain large stacks of military and other records pertaining to the nineteenth and twentieth centuries. They are in English and Urdu and are for the most part uncatalogued. It is very likely that, if examined carefully, they would reveal much about Africans in the Deccan. I did not make an exhaustive examination of that collection. Another valuable collection of relevant materials is located in the archives at Poona.

Another important primary source is the archival collection at Goa. As headquarters for Portuguese East African interests, Goa dispatched merchants, soldiers, and missionaries to various parts of East Africa for over 300 years, during which time many Africans entered Diu and Goa as servants and slaves. I did not see this collection but examined P. S. Pissurlencar's catalogue, *Roteiro dos Arquivos da India Portuguesa* (1955), which is a very helpful guide to much of the material. The catalogue's main weakness, however, is its failure to supply specific descriptions of the material in the archives. For example, some volumes are simply listed under the heading "Slave Trade and Mozambique"; one would have to go through the volumes to determine what aspects of the slave trade are included. Still, the possibility of productive research in Goa is great indeed.

Secondary Sources. There are three books on slavery in India in which Africans receive very brief mention: D. R. Banaji, *Slavery in*

British India (Bombay, 1933); Dev Raj Chanana, *Slavery in Ancient India* (New Delhi, 1960); and Amal Kumar Chattopadhyay, *Slavery in India* (Calcutta, 1959). There are several standard and lesser-known books on Indian history which mention and, in some cases, briefly discuss certain aspects of the African presence in India: John Briggs, *History of the Rise of the Mohamedan Power in India* (London, 1829); *The Cambridge History of India* (London, 1937), Vols. III, IV; M. S. Commissariat, *A History of Gujarat*, Vol. II (Calcutta, 1957); H. M. Elliot and J. Dowson, *History of India As Told by Its Own Historians* (London, 1867); James Fergusson, *History of Indian and Eastern Architecture*, ed. James Burgess (Delhi, 1967); James Fergusson and Theodore Hope, *Architecture of Ahmadabad* (London, 1866); J. D. B. Gribble, *A History of the Deccan* (London, 1896); Ratnamanirao B. Jhote, *Ahmadabad* (n.p., n.d.); *Lalit Kala: A Journal of Oriental Art, Chiefly Indian*, nos. 1, 2 (April, 1955; March, 1956); S. Lane-Poole, *The Muhammadan Dynasties* (London, 1894); R. C. Majumdar, *The History and Culture of the Indian People: The Delhi Sultanate* (Bombay, 1960), and *An Advanced History of India* (London, 1950); K. M. Panikkar, *India and the Indian Ocean* (London, 1945); J. C. Powell-Price, *A History of India* (London, 1955); E. Dension Ross, *An Arabic History of Gujarat*, Vol. II (London, 1921); Jadunath Sarkar, *History of Aurangzib*, Vol. IV (Calcutta, 1919), and *Shivaji and His Times* (Calcutta, 1920); Radhey Shyam, *The Kingdom of Ahmadnagar* (New Delhi, 1966).

It should be noted that the standard translations of the Persian documents, on which most if not all of the above books rely heavily, are at Aligarh University in India. Since those translations are old and were completed when African studies in general were not regarded as important research endeavors, at least a re-evaluation and perhaps even a fresh translation should be undertaken in the light of new information and different perspectives. There is also a need to search for locally published materials in Indian languages. Sheikh Chand, *Malik Ambar* (Hyderabad, 1931) is only one example of what may be expected from this approach.

There are numerous travel accounts in which occasional references to Africans in Asia are made, but what one finds may not be as substantive as desired. The following works provide especially helpful information on the African slave trade and the locations of Africans in parts of Asia. The accounts of several travelers are included in John Pinkerton, ed., *A General Collection of the Best and Most Interesting Voyages and Travels in All Parts of the World* (London, 1811). A fairly detailed description of a caravan with slaves traveling from Ethiopia to Delhi may be found in François Bernier, *Travels in the Moghul Empire, 1656–1668* (London, 1916). Other useful references to Africans in Indian history are: Richard F. Burton, *Scinde, or the Unhappy Valley* (London, 1851), Vol. I, and *Sind Revisited* (London, 1872), Vols. I, II; H. A. R. Gibb, *The Travels of Ibn Battuta* (New York, 1929) ; John Henry Grose, *A Voyage to the East Indies* (London, 1751) ; and George Valentia, *Voyages and Travels to India, Ceylon, the Red Sea, Abyssinia and Egypt*, 3 Vols. (London, 1851).

Indispensable sources of Indian history are the gazetteers, which survey the history of particular provinces. Several of the gazetteers contain scattered but useful references and short accounts of African activities in India. The most helpful gazetteers for this book were: India: *Imperial Gazetteer of India, Bombay Presidency* (Calcutta, 1909), Vol. II; India, *Gazetteer of Bombay City and Island* (Bombay, 1909), Vol. I; Bombay, *Gazetteer of the Bombay Presidency, Kolaba and Janjira* (Bombay, 1883) ; Bombay, *Gazetteer of the Bombay Presidency, Ahmedabad* (Bombay, 1884) ; Bombay, *Gazetteer of the Bombay Presidency, Aurangabad* (Bombay, 1884). These gazetteers are readily available in several libraries in New Delhi and Bombay.

It is not surprising that Malik Ambar is the one African in Indian history who has received the greatest amount of scholarly attention. Two small books and a few articles have examined the era of his reign. Sheikh Chand, *Malik Ambar* (Hyderabad, 1931) is in Urdu and seems to be the most available; a copy is located in the library of the University of Bombay. I was not able to locate the second book, J. N. Chaudhuri, *Malik Ambar* (Calcutta, n.d.), but I did discuss it with persons who had read it. Of the two books, I was told, Chand's has the greater amount of substance and is more reliable. There have been several articles written about Malik Ambar. Bena Rasi Prasad Saksena, "Malik Ambar," *Hindustani Academy*, no. 4 (October,

1933), is written in Hindi. Two others are: Gulam Ahmad Khan, "The History of the City of Aurangabad," in *Transactions of the Indian History Congress* (Hyderabad, 1941); and D. R. Seth, "The Life and Times of Malik Ambar," *Islamic Culture: An English Quarterly*, Vol. XXXI (Hyderabad, January, 1957).

There is one book on the Siddis: D. R. Banaji, *Bombay and the Siddis* (Bombay, 1932). This book examines the relationship between the Siddis, primarily those of Janjira, and the establishment of Bombay under the British. Banaji's book and the doctoral dissertation of R. V. Ramdas, "Relations between the Marathas and the Siddis of Janjira" (University of Bombay, n.d.), are essentially studies of the political activities of the Janjira Siddis.

INDEX

Abhangar Khan, 92

Abolition, 6, 7, 8, 51, 52, 53, 54, 58, 59; Treaty of (1873), 10, 17, 18, 54, 61, 63, 65

Abu Bakr, 30

Abu l'Makarim Mujir al Din, 78

Abyssinia, 130, 131

Abyssinian: merchants in Gujarat, 87; prisoners in Gujarat, 87; servants, 70; slave markets, 22; slaves, 82, 89

Abyssinians, 49, 70, 73, 75, 80, 81, 83, 88, 97, 100

Aden, xii, 22, 30, 61, 66, 67, 68, 71, 76, 105, 107, 108, 130

Aden, Gulf of, 16, 35, 44, 46, 47

Africa, xi, xii, xiv, 3, 6, 8, 31, 34, 36, 37, 38, 48, 50, 51, 54, 58, 59, 61, 68, 72, 75, 81, 108, 112, 113, 117, 119, 120, 121, 122, 126, 127; relations with outside world, 118

African: ancestry, 26, 89, 106, 113, 114; coast, 23, 75; consciousness, 126; culture and its retention, 112, 120, 122, 124; descendants, xi, xii, xiv, 76, 77, 78, 87, 90, 92, 99, 100, 106, 111, 114, 118, 120 n, 125, 126, 127; diaspora, xiv, 3, 43, 115; heritage, 97, 120, 123; immigration, 99, 105, 115, 117; labor, 8, 119; languages, 122; migration, 100, 110, 114; ports, 13, 60; settle-

ments in India and Iran, 77, 78, 87, 114, 118, 124

African Asylum in Nasik, 72, 74, 75, 76

African Cavalry Guard in Hyderabad, 103-8, 111; origin of, 106; recruitment and training of, 103; terms of service for, 104; status of, 124; disbanded, 124

Africans, xi, xii, xiii, xiv, xv, 6, 8, 10, 13, 19, 23, 31, 33, 35, 37, 38, 39, 40, 41, 49, 50, 53, 54, 55, 56, 57, 59, 64, 66, 67, 68, 69, 70, 72, 73, 75, 76, 78, 80, 82, 91, 94, 97, 98, 103, 104, 105, 115, 122, 123, 125, 126; mercenaries, 87, 88, 92; merchants, 12, 77; priests, 81; slave-soldiers, 5, 79, 92, 99; sovereigns, 14; teachers, 74, 81, 89, 90, 99, 100, 101, 102, 110, 111, 112, 114, 118, 119, 120, 121, 124, 127

Afro-Americans, 125, 126, 127

Afro-Asians, 115, 119, 122, 123, 125, 126, 127; heritage of, xii

Afro-Indians, 76, 90, 114, 117

Agra, 70, 89

Ahmadabad, 88, 89

Ahmadnagar, 72, 81, 82, 92, 93, 96, 98, 121

Ahmed bin Alia Aseeree, 101

Ahmed Nizam Shah, 89

Ajawa, 12, 18

147

Alamayu, 109 n
Alexandria, 38
Ali Mookaree, 101
Ambar Geshen, 121
Amharic, 109
Amir-ul-Umara Malik Andil (Indil Khan), 79, 80
Angola, 7
Ankole, 12
Arab: cities and towns, 15, 52; dhows, 52, 100 n, 102; slave vessels, 52, 71
Arabia, xi, 5, 15, 23, 27, 30, 31, 34, 43, 48, 52, 53, 61, 67, 81, 95, 101, 102, 103, 104, 106, 108, 113, 114, 122; cities and towns of, 3, 36, 37; coast of, 10; ports in, 72, 82; slave markets in, 36, 64; slave recruitment in, 111; territories of, 53
Arabic, xiii, 20, 63, 71, 77, 80, 92, 96, 104, 108, 122
Arabs, xiii, 3, 5, 6, 7, 12, 13, 14, 16, 17, 19, 22, 24, 30, 31, 35, 40, 53, 54, 62, 65, 70, 87, 91, 96, 107, 108, 110, 121, 123, 127; in the Deccan, 92, 95, 99; in Gujarat, 87; in Hyderabad, 101, 102, 103, 104, 112, 113, 114, 124; merchants, 14, 27, 35, 100; slave dealers, 8, 12, 23, 33, 101
Aryans, 115, 116, 118
Asad Beg, 95
Asia, xi, xii, xiii, xiv, xv, 3, 5, 8, 30, 33, 35, 36, 39, 41, 43, 49, 51, 54, 64, 65, 66, 76, 81, 87, 99, 100, 112, 115, 118, 119, 120, 121, 125, 126, 127; Africans in, 127; demand for slaves in, 8, 52; ports in, 27, 48, 60; slave markets in, 27, 50
Asirgarh, 121
Aslam, Reuben, 101
Assab, 30
Assimilation, 114, 121–22
Atlantic Ocean, xiii, 7, 8
Aurangabad, 101. See also Nasik

Bab el Mandeb Strait, 27, 30
Bagamoyo, 19, 30, 55, 120
Baghdad, 38, 39, 66, 91
Bahmani: kingdom, 102; kings, 5

Bahrein, 5, 36, 37, 38, 39, 48, 66
Bahr el Ghazal, 11, 16, 44
Baker, C. J., 61, 108
Balfour, E. G., 101
Baluchistan, 77
Banaji, D. R., 81
Bandar Abbas, 5, 36, 37, 39, 48, 66, 77, 78, 118
Bandra, 72
Banians, 13, 62
Baratieri, Oreste, 46
Barbak Shah (Sultan Shahzada), 79
Baroda, 34
Basra, 5, 15, 38, 39, 48, 49, 66, 70
Bastani-Parizi, E., 77
Batinah coast, 5, 37, 39, 60, 61, 120, 131, 132
Beckingham, C. F., 121
Bedouins, 61
Beilul, 16, 27, 30, 36, 46, 47
Beke, C. T., 44
Bengal, 79, 80, 123; Siddis in, 127
Bengali Africans, 123
Benghazi, 8, 38
Benjamin, William, 75
Berbera, 3, 5, 47
Berlin Conference of 1884–85, 59
Berlioux, E. F., 46
Bernier, François, 34, 35
Bertrand Franch Mahé de la Bourdonnais, 8
Béteille, André, 116
Bidar, 114
Bijapur, 83, 92, 94
Bilal, 96, 122
Bilal bin Mabrook, 111 n
Bisa, 14
Blackness, 97, 116; stigma against, 115, 117, 118
Blue Nile, 16, 44
Bohra Muhammadbhai Alibhai, 63
Bombay, 34, 54, 55, 56, 62, 66, 68, 69, 70, 71, 76, 80, 84, 85, 107, 108, 123, 124, 130, 133; Africans detained at, 104; census of, 72; customs officials at, 101; depot for freed Africans at, 74; government of, 6, 72, 74, 86; police commissioner of, 72, 74, 119; Siddis of, 123, 124; slave trade to, 100, 102

"Bombay Africans," 55, 126
Bondsmen, 7, 51, 53, 69, 76. *See also*
    Slaves
Bonga, 11, 44
Brahmin, 95, 115; black, 116
Brava, 5, 19, 31
Brazil, 7
Britain, xii, 7, 10, 17, 23, 51, 52, 53,
    58, 65, 66, 74, 75, 85, 86, 106, 117
British: Anti-Slavery Society, 54;
    East India Company, xiv, 66, 68,
    69, 82, 84, 85; expedition to Ethi-
    opia (1868), 67, 106, 107, 108, 110;
    government, 54, 63, 84, 86, 89, 110;
    India, 6, 52; Indian army, 102;
    merchants, 63; naval cruisers and
    commanders, 7, 13, 24, 30, 31, 32,
    33, 36, 52, 54, 57, 61, 66, 68; proc-
    lamation against slavery (1839),
    71; Slave Squadron, 7; trade with
    Janjira, 86; treasury, 55, 66
Broach, 34
Brucks, G. B., 49
Brussels Conference of 1889, 58–60
Bunyoro, 12
Burton, Richard, 90
Bushire, 36, 37, 48, 49

Calcutta, 35
Caste, 116, 117
Cecchi, Antonio, 11, 44
Chesney, George, 105
Chingiz Khan, 92, 94
Chingula, Don Jeronimo, 82 n
Christianity, 53, 54, 59
Christians, xii, 52, 53, 54, 56, 59, 71,
    72, 80, 107, 124
Chuma, 75
Church Missionary Society (CMS),
    55, 57, 72, 74, 75
Church of Scotland mission (Aden),
    67
Coghlan, William M., 10, 22, 47
Colomb, P., 31
Commissariat, M. S., 89
Concubines, 5, 119
Congo, 12, 15
Constantinople, 66, 87
Council of the United Merchants of
    England, 68

Coupland, Reginald, 3
Cox, P. Z., 64
Curzon, Lord, 89
Cutch, 12, 14, 49, 52, 62, 63, 70, 90,
    137; captured slaves in, 135; slave
    trade to, 100
Cutchees, 62, 63

Dacca, 35
Dallons, P., 6
D'Almeida, Nicolau Tolentino, 8
Danakil country, 16
Dar es Salaam, 17, 19, 55, 119, 120,
    131, 132
Darfur, 11, 14
Darrison, Baron, 9
Daulatabad, 94
Deccan, 5, 82, 91, 92, 93, 94, 95, 97,
    98, 99, 103, 123
Deh-Zanjian, 77
Delgado, Cape, 52
Delhi, 78, 84, 89, 105, 112
Denmark, 51
De Sarzec, Consul, 46
Dhalak, 5
Dhows, xiii, 20, 27, 30, 31, 36, 37, 39,
    40, 61, 66, 70; crews on, 5; de-
    scription of, 13, 31; slave condi-
    tions on, 20, 32–33
Diu, 34, 52, 81, 88, 100 n; slave
    trade to, 100
Domestics, 58, 75, 81; servants, 5,
    112, 114; slaves, 101
Dowson, J., 97
DuBois, W. E. B., 125 n
Duse Mohamed, 125 n

East Africa, xiii, 3, 5, 6, 7, 8, 10, 11,
    24, 27, 34, 36, 43, 48, 50, 51, 52,
    53, 55, 58, 62, 64, 65, 75, 84, 106,
    117, 122
East African: coast, 6, 19, 20, 27, 55,
    66, 74; colonies, 81; merchants,
    77; ports, 30, 81; slave trade, 32,
    100, 106; slaves, 10
East India Company, 85. *See also*
    British East India Company
Education, 20, 25; of khanazahs,
    103; of liberated Africans, 56–57
Egerton, E. H., 61

Egypt, 5, 8, 11, 23, 37, 44, 125 n
Egyptian: armies, 11; orders for
slaves, 46; slave markets, 11;
soldiers, 11; steamers, 32, 33
Elliott, H. M., 97
El Obeid, 14, 15
Elton, Frederic, 16, 17, 18, 20, 45
Engagé system, 9–10
Entoto, 16
Ethiopia, 6, 11, 14, 16, 23, 35, 43,
44, 91, 106, 107, 108, 109, 110, 119,
121, 122; merchants of, 77; Muslim invasion of, in 1527, 87. *See
also* Abyssinia
Ethiopian: campaign of 1868, 108;
code, 6; kings, 34–35; merchants,
34; migration to and settlement in
India, 109–10; slave routes, 16
Ethiopians, 70, 78, 96 n, 106, 107, 121
Euphrates River, 38
Europe, xiii, xiv, 3, 7, 8, 15, 19, 22,
25, 35, 38, 51, 53, 54, 57, 69, 73, 85,
100, 117, 118, 119, 120, 126
European: clipper ships, 20; demand
for slaves, 7; explorers, 33; families, 73; merchants, 56; missionaries, 33, 43; slave vessels, 3, 33,
84; travelers, 43

Farquhar, Robert, 52
Fergusson, James, 88
Ferista, 78, 97
Fetha nagast, 6
Fettah Khan, 94
Fiji Islands, 73
Fontanier, V., 49
France, xii, 7, 53, 117
Freedmen, 34, 56, 57, 66–68, 69, 72,
73, 75, 76; depots for, 71, 72; edu-
cation of, 55, 56, 57; employment
of, 66, 67, 72, 75–76, 78; settle-
ments of, 56, 67, 74, 75; welfare of,
66, 71, 72, 73, 102, 110, 124. *See
also* Liberated Africans
Freeman-Grenville, G. S. P., 3
French: colonies, 17, 61, 64; *engagé*
system, 10, 53; government, 10;
slave trade policy, 60; slave ves-
sels, 8, 10, 59–63
Frere, Bartle, 54, 55, 56, 58, 75

Freretown, 55, 56, 75
Furrege bin Buckree, 108

Gala-Zanjian, 77
Galla, 14, 16, 122
Gallabat, 14
Garvey, Marcus, 125 n
Gir forest, 90
Goa, xiv, 81, 100 n, 107; slave trade
to, 100
Gojam, 130
Gokaldass, Kesu, 63
Golconda, 92, 94
Gold Coast, 7
Gondar, 11, 107
Good Hope, Cape of, 72
Gorden, Arthur, 56
Gordon, Charles G., 11, 44
Greece, xiii
Guardafui, Cape, 19
Guardsmen, 112. *See also* African
Cavalry Guard in Hyderabad
Gujarat, 5, 34, 82, 87–90, 92; armies
of, 87; language of, 63, 71; news-
papers of, 63
Gurage, 11, 44, 119, 130

Habesh Khan, 80
Habshi Guda, 114
Habshis, 39, 49, 50, 78, 81, 87, 88, 92,
93, 95, 98; army of, 92, 95; com-
munity of, 87; defined, 16 n; in
Gujarat, 88; in Jedda, 101; in
Khandesh, 121; rebellion and re-
volt of, in Ahmadnagar, 88, 92;
slave dealers in Hyderabad, 101;
slaves, 88, 92, 95
Hajji-ad-Dabir, 87
Harar, 16, 91
Hardinge, A. H., 55
Harris, William C., 19, 44, 46
Haussman, A., 45
Hejaz, 91
Henderson, J., 72
Heuglin, T., 45
Hill, Captain, 108
Hindus, 35, 63, 80, 96, 116, 117, 120;
boys, 74; merchants, 13; in the
Deccan, 95; rulers, 103; slave girls,
101

Hindustani, 75
Hodeida, 27, 30, 36, 49
Holmwood Report, 17
Hormuz, 77
Houssain Rudaaee, 101
Hyderabad (city), 100–104, 107, 108, 110–13, 121, 124; African community in, 124; employment opportunities for Africans in, 114; military forces of, 102; nizam of, 103, 112, 113; Siddis of, 123, 124

Iberian peninsula, xiii
Ibo, 18, 19, 30
Ibrahim Adil Shah II, 94
Ifag, 44
Ikhtiyar Khan, 89
Ikhtiyar-ul-Mulk, 88
Imperial Service Troops of India, 105
India, xi, xii, xiii, 5, 6, 34, 36, 39, 43, 49, 52, 57, 63, 64, 69, 70, 73, 77–82, 84–87, 90–92, 95, 99, 100, 105, 109, 110, 112, 113, 115–18, 121–23; architecture of, 88; cities of, 101; Government Act of 1843, 52; government of, 64, 68, 104, 105, 109, 110, 113; independence of, 113; merchants of, 60, 77; navy of, 34, 72; newspapers of, 112, 116; Republic Day (1953), 112; slave trade to, 106
Indian Ocean, xii, xiii, 5, 8, 32, 40, 43, 52, 53, 66, 83, 87
Indians, 13, 35, 62, 63, 69, 72, 73, 74, 81, 82, 83, 85, 98, 99, 101, 105, 112, 113, 114, 115, 118, 124; involvement in slave trade, 12, 23, 62, 64, 84, 101
India Office (London), 61
Indra, 116
Iran, xii, 77, 78, 115; African communities in, 77, 78, 118; racialism in, 118
Iranians, 77, 78, 118
Iraq, xii, 39
Isfahan, 78 n, 118
Islam, xiii, 5, 35, 39, 51, 80, 86, 96, 98, 107, 111, 112, 121–23; appeal of, 121; assimilative character of,

122, 123, 125, 126; as "black man's religion," 122; heritage of, 127
Ismail Fuquchee, 101

Jaffer Yab Khan, 89
Jaipur, 70, 108
Jalal-ud-din Fath Shah, 79
Jalal-ud-din Yacut, 78
Janjero, 81 n
Janjira, 80–87, 93, 123; census of, 80; economy of, 87; nawabs of, 80, 86; navy of, 83, 85
Jaunpur, 79
Jedda, 27, 30, 36, 37, 49, 101, 119, 130, 131
Jeffries, Robert, 82
Jews, 80
Jhujhar Khan, 88
Jibuti, 16
Jimma, 11, 44
Jiruft, 77; community of African descent in, 118
Jodia, 63
Johanna Island, 58

Kaffa, 44
Kalachabutra, 96
Kalamajid, 96
Kamba, 14
Karachi, 49, 70, 74, 90
Karagwe, 15
Karikal, 9
Kassala, 14
Kathiawar, 34, 49, 52, 62, 63, 71; number of slaves in, 70; slave trade to, 100
Kazi Hussein, 91, 92, 94
Kemball, A. B., 48
Kengia, Mfumwa, 14, 24
Kenya, 14, 126
Kenyatta, Jomo, 126
Kerman, 77
Khanazahs, 103, 104, 114, 125
Khandesh, 72; Habshis in, 121
Khartoum, 14
Khayrat Khan, 87
Khvaja Jahan (Malik Sarvar), 78
Khwanze Humayun, 92
Kilwa, 6, 8, 17, 22, 30, 47, 48, 56, 120, 132, 133; slave market in, 20

Kimaneta, 12
Kipsigis, 12
Kiriche, 14, 24
Kirk, John, 16, 17
Kirkee, 93, 93 n, 96, 97
Kobishanow, Yu. M., xii
Konkan, 80, 81, 82, 83
Koran, 121
Koranic: education, 95, 125; school,
    111
Kordofan, 11, 14, 15, 19
Krapf, John, 11, 43, 44
Krishna, 116
Kuwait, 36, 38, 48

Laaeed bin Hameed, 101
Lamu, 17, 19, 31, 56
Leakey, Louis, xii
Liberated Africans, 33, 54, 55, 56,
    57, 58, 67, 68, 72, 74, 100 n, 102,
    119, 123, 124; in Bombay, 73;
    communities and settlements of,
    58, 65; depots for, 66, 68; educa-
    tion of, 55, 56, 57; in Nasik, 74;
    Siddi descendants of, 123. See also
    Freedmen
Liberia, 55, 58
Lingeh, 5, 36, 37, 38, 39, 48
Livingstone, David, 15, 16, 45, 53,
    54, 75
Lucknow, 35, 70

Mackenzie, T., 49
MacLeod, Lyons, 47, 48
Madagascar, 8, 19, 30, 60, 61, 63, 68
Madonda, 12, 18
Mafia Island, 17
Magdala, 106, 109
Mahé (Seychelles), 57
Mahmud III (Gujarat), 88
Mahomed bin Noor, 108
Mahomed bin Sayeed, 108
Majumdar, R. C., 78, 79, 99
Makonde, 12, 18
Makua, 12, 18
Malabar Coast, 70, 100
Malik Ambar, 82, 83, 91, 92, 93, 94,
    96, 97, 98, 102 n, 120, 123, 127;
    administration of, 94–95; alliance
    with Janjiran Siddis, 125; army of,

93; cultural achievements of, 96;
    death of, 94; historians praise,
    97–98
Malik Qaranful, 79
Malik-ush Sharq (Malik Sarvar), 78,
    79
Malindi, 19, 120, 131
Mandal Dilawar Khan, 87
Mandavie, 137
Mangu, 122
Manumission, 54, 66, 71, 76, 120,
    121; details of, 65–66
Marathas, 82, 83, 84, 95, 123
Marathi, 71, 75, 80, 96
Masailand, 12
Mascarene Islands, 6, 8, 53
Massaia, Guglielmo, 44
Massawa, 5, 16, 22, 35, 45, 46, 47
Matamba, 18
Mateb, 109
Mathew, Gervase, 3, 5
Mauritius, 8, 52, 56, 57, 66
Mazrui dynasty, 7
Mecca, 35, 36, 38, 100, 101, 105, 130,
    131
Mediterranean Sea, 38
Merca, 5, 19
Mercenaries, African, 92, 101
Meshesha, 106, 107, 108, 109, 110
Mesopotamia, 5, 39
Mian Raju Dakhani, 93
Middle Ages, 5, 35, 78, 99, 102
Middle East, 6, 8
Minab, 5, 39, 77
Mirambo, 14
Mirza Muhammad Hadi, 98
Missionaries, xiv, 45, 53, 54, 55, 75;
    European, 126; schools and sta-
    tions of, 67, 72, 73
Mlozi, 15
Mocha, 27, 34, 36, 69, 70, 91, 129
Mogadishu, 5, 19
Mohumorah, 48
Mombasa, 7, 8, 17, 19, 55, 56, 75, 136,
    137
Mon Plaisir, 56
Monsoons, 19, 27, 36, 66
Moobarick bin Mooullin, 101
Moresby, Fairfax, 20, 32
Moresby Treaty of 1822, 52, 54

Morice, Captain, 8
Mosaic law, 6
Mozambique, 7, 8, 10, 19, 24, 30, 34, 47, 48, 56, 61, 75, 81, 100 n, 106
Mughuls, 34, 70, 82, 83, 84, 88, 91, 93, 94, 95, 97, 99, 103, 125; Akbar, 88, 93; armies of, 82, 84; Aurangzib, 34, 35; Jahangir, 93, 97, 98; merchants, 70; Shah Jahan, 94
Mukalla, 36, 52
Mulattoes, 14, 24
Munjee, Kanru, 62
Munzinger, Werner, 46
Murtaza I of Ahmadnagar, 92
Murtaza II of Ahmadnagar, 93
Muscat, 6, 7, 20, 31, 36, 37, 48, 49, 52, 54, 62, 64, 66, 69, 70, 73, 81, 101; slave merchants in, 100; slave vessels of, 52
Muslim: Africans, 35, 71; architecture, 89; Indians, 63, 99; invasion of Ethiopia (1527), 87; pilgrims, 83; provinces of Persia, 91; slave dealers, 101, 121; theology, 121
Muslims, xiii, 5, 34, 35, 36, 39, 56, 72, 78, 80, 98, 102, 104, 109, 111, 115, 120, 121, 122, 124; deported from India, 113
Mustafa bin-Bahram, 87
Myseram Regiment, 108

Nakhuda Mhala, 96
Nasik, 55, 66, 72, 74, 75, 76
Nasir bin Muftah, 103, 113
Nasr-ud-din Mahmud, 80
Navanagar, 63, 64
Netherlands, 86, 117
Ngindo, 12
Nile Valley, 8, 11; slave trade in, 23
Nizam mul-Mulk Bani, 92
Nizam Shahi kingdom, 98
Nkrumah, Kwame, 125 n
North Borneo Company, 73
Nyamwezi, 14, 24
Nyanja, 12
Nyasa, Lake, 12, 14, 15, 17, 18, 45

Oasim Khan, 89
Obok, 60

Oman, 3, 5, 6, 12, 20, 37, 51, 52, 53, 60, 61
Oman, Gulf of, 31, 37
O'Neill, Henry, 18, 45
Opone, 5
Ottavi, M. P., 60
Oudh, 70

Pakistan, xii, 34, 113
Pallme, Ignacius, 15
Pan-African: conference, 125; movement, 125, 126; unity, 125
Pangani, 17, 18, 19, 30
Pankhurst, Richard, 48, 121
Pearl-diving, 5, 37, 38, 38 n, 119
Pemba, 6, 19, 56
Perim, 30
Periplus, 3, 81
Persia, 5, 52, 60, 90, 95, 96, 99, 122, 123
Persian: culture and history, 118; empire, 90; language, 71, 77, 96
Persian Gulf, xi, xiii, 5, 6, 23, 27, 31, 34, 37, 38, 39, 40, 43, 48, 49, 52, 60, 61, 64, 70, 71, 73, 78, 90, 95, 101, 118; ports of, 72; slave markets along, 64; towns of, 36
Pilgrimages to Mecca, 36, 100, 105
Plantations, 56, 57; clove, 6, 7; date, 5, 37, 39, 78, 119; economy of, 8; labor for, 55
Pondicherry, 9
Poona, 72, 133
Porbandar, 34, 71
Portugal, 47, 86, 87, 117
Portuguese: East Africa, 10; explorers, xiv; India, 83; Mozambique, 7, 18, 56; slave ports, 100 n
Price, William S., 55, 72, 74
Prideaux, W. F., 37, 57, 108, 109, 110

Quelimane, 18, 19

Race: beliefs about, xii, 99, 117, 118; myths about, 115, 117, 118; stereotypes of, 100, 113, 115, 117, 118
Racism, 97, 126, 127
Ramadan, 56
Ras al Hadd, 30
Ras Ali, 107

Ras Assir, 5
Ras Rasheim, 120, 133
Raziya, Queen, 78
Red Sea, xiii, 16, 22, 23, 30, 31, 32, 33, 35, 36, 38, 40, 43, 44, 45, 46, 52, 66, 71; ports of, 11, 47, 48
Reduit, 56
Réunion: French settlers on, 8, 10; slaves imported into, 10
Richard, Henri, 56
Rigby, Christopher, 10, 19, 20, 21, 45, 47, 62
Rig-Veda, 116
Robertson, A. D., 37, 101
Rogge, 44
Roheita, 16, 27, 30, 35, 46, 47
Rudolph, Lake, 12
Rukn-ud-din Barbak, 79
Runtoné, M., 9
Russell, Lord John, 10
Ruvuma River, 12, 18, 56

Sachin, 89
Sadani, 17
Said ibn Ahmad, 6
Said Majid, 63
Salar Jang I, 102
Salar Jung, 102
Salisbury, Lord, 55
Salt, Henry, 22
Secunderabad-Hyderabad, 101
Sennar, 14, 129
Seth, D. R., 98
Seychelles, 66, 71
Shahzada, 79
Shaik Mohamed, 101
Shams-ud-din Abu Nasr Muzaffar Shah (Sidi Badr), 80
Shams-ud-din Ibrahim, 79
Sharjah, 37, 132
Sheik Sayeed al-Habshi Sultani, 88
Shendi, 14
Shi'ites, 99
Shili Trimi, 96
Shiraz, 78, 118
Shivaji, 83
Shoa, 11, 16, 44, 46
Shyam, Radhey, 98
Siddi Ahmad Khan, 82

Siddi Ahmed Khan, 86
Siddi Bashire, 89
Siddi Ibrahim Khan, 86
Siddi Kasim, 84
Siddi Masud, 85
Siddi Risala, 99–114, 124, 125; administration of, 111; African origins of, 114; economic activities in, 111; population of, 114; social life in, 111–14
Siddis, 40, 50, 69, 80, 81, 82, 83, 84, 85, 86, 87, 113; dancers, 112, 121; defined, 39 n; in Hyderabad, 103, 104, 106, 111, 113, 114, 121, 125, 127; in Janjira, 80–87, 93, 123, 125, 127; navy of, 84, 85, 123; nawabs, 80, 81; nobles, 80, 86; seamen, 82; soldiers, 81, 84
Siddi Sa'id's mosque, 88
Siddi Shamshir Khan, 89
Siddi Yacoot Khan, 86
Sidi Badr, 80
Sierra Leone, 55
Sind, 34, 49
Siroor (Poona), American mission in, 72
Slaves, xiii, 3, 5, 32, 53, 55, 57, 58, 62, 69–71, 74, 97, 98, 122, 126; in Bombay, 102; caravans of, 6, 7, 12, 13, 14, 17, 18, 19, 23, 39, 44, 46, 59; dealers of, xiii, 4, 6, 8, 11, 12, 13, 14, 15, 18, 20, 22, 24, 30, 31, 36, 38, 43, 50, 63, 65, 70, 92, 101; demand for, 15, 23, 40, 51, 65; depots for, 8, 12, 18, 19, 30, 36, 37, 38; dhows used to transport, 36–37, 60; duties of, 23, 31, 35, 36, 37, 38, 39–41, 46, 56, 70, 78, 79, 119; hired, 31, 37, 39, 68; in Hyderabad, 101, 102, 110; imported into Asia, 35, 37, 49, 52, 59, 60, 61, 70, 81; in India, 70, 78, 81, 105; in Iran, 77, 78; kidnapings and raids of, 11, 12, 13, 18, 19, 23, 24, 27, 120; march of, to coastal markets, 13, 15, 16, 17, 18, 19, 20, 27, 30, 34, 36, 38, 43, 44, 45, 46, 50, 61, 120; markets for, 6, 11, 13, 14, 19–23, 24, 35–39, 43, 44, 45, 50, 52,

54, 68–70; sources of, 7, 10–15, 24, 38, 43–48, 52, 64, 65; statements of, 33, 49, 65, 119, 129–33; treatment of, 40–41, 65, 121
Slave trade, xiii, xiv, 5–8, 10–11, 13, 22–25, 33–34, 36–38, 40, 51–54, 58–64, 68, 70, 81, 101, 106, 117, 118; restriction and abolition of, 3, 11, 16, 17, 18, 23, 30, 31, 32, 33, 36, 45, 46, 52, 54, 59, 60, 61, 63, 64, 65, 66, 69, 71, 74, 100; revenue from, 4, 7, 8, 12, 16, 18, 20, 22, 23, 53; routes of, xi, 7, 14, 15, 17, 18, 19, 37, 45, 61; volume of, 43, 45, 47, 48, 49
Smee, T., 6
Smith, James, 72
Socotra Island, 52
Sofala, 19, 81
Soleillet, Paul, 46
Soliaman bin Haftoo, 106, 107, 108, 109, 110
Somalia, 17, 19, 75; coast of, 3, 5, 11, 32, 56; Islam in, 122; kings of, 20; slaves from, 56
Sotik, 12
South Africa, 58
Stace, Colonel, 22
Straits Settlement in Fiji and Sarawak, 73
Suakin, 5, 14, 35, 47, 129
Sudan, 11, 14, 23, 44, 122
Sulivan, G. L., 32
Sunnites, 99, 99 n, 111
Sur, 36, 37, 49, 60, 61, 64, 132
Surat, 34, 69, 85, 89; rulers of, 84, 85
Swahili: language, 61, 111, 112, 121; slave caravan assistants, 23; slave dhows, 30; towns, 52
Syed bin Rujjub, 108
Syed Monjut, 107
Synd Hussin bin Uhmud Hubushee, 69

Tabora, 14
Tajura, 5, 22, 27, 30, 36, 46, 47, 61
Tajura, Gulf of, 16, 22
Tana River, 12

Tanganyika, Lake, 14, 15
Tanzania, 5, 14, 17, 19, 24, 45
Tawabatch, 107
Tegbakt, 84
Tehran, 118
Theodore (Ethiopian emperor), 106, 107, 108, 109
Tigre, 16
Tigris River, 38
Tippu Tib, 14, 15
Toro, 12
Trinity Chapel, 74
Tripoli, 8, 38
Tulshi Narsi, 63
Turkana, 12
Turkey, xii, 38
Turkish: Arabia, 39, 101; authorities, 30; slave demand and supply, 38; steamers, 33; tobacco company, 63
Turks, 30, 70, 99
Tweedie, W., 102

Uganda, 24
Uhmud bin Salim Noemin, 69
United States, xi, xiii, 3, 7, 51, 53, 100, 117; racism in, 126; black power movements in, 127
Universities Mission, 55
University of Bombay, 74
University of Tehran, 77
Ulugh Khan (Yacut Sabit Khan Habshi), 87
Urdu, 112

Victoria, Lake, 12
Victoria, Queen, 106

Wanparthy, raja of, 102, 103
Waq, 122
Wasseen, 17
Wellington, Mathew, 55, 75
West Africa, xiii, 7, 8, 50, 51, 53, 55, 58, 126
West Indies, 126; racism in, 126; black power movements in, 127
Willoughby, I. P., 70
Wilson, David, 48, 49
Winsor, R., 72

Yacoob, 101
Yacut Sabit Khan Habshi, 87
Yao, 14, 24, 133
Yemen, xii

Zaid-ibn-Khalifa, 38
Zanjiabad, 77

Zanzibar, 3, 6, 7, 10, 12, 13, 17, 19,
    20, 21, 22, 23, 27, 30, 31, 33, 37,
    44, 45, 47, 48, 49, 52, 53, 54, 55,
    56, 57, 60, 61, 62, 63, 75, 100, 106,
    120, 133, 135, 136, 137
Zeila, 3, 5, 16, 22, 36, 46, 47
Zubair, 38